Stealing the Mississippi River

Fascinating History of the
La Crescent, Minnesota Area

Donna Christoph Huegel

Lovstad Publishing
www.Lovstadpublishing.com
Baraboo, WI/Yuma, AZ

STEALING THE MISSISSIPPI RIVER

First Edition

ISBN: 0-9749058-4-4
ISBN-13: 978-0974905846
Printed in the United States of America

Also by Donna Huegel
MANY A GROVE AND ORCHARD
The Story of John S. Harris

This book is dedicated to
my husband, Len,
and sons, Eric and Ryan
who are the sunshine of my life.

ACKNOWLEDGEMENTS

There are many people I wish to thank for making this book possible. First of all, I thank the La Crescent Area Historical Society and its many contributions of information and artifacts, and the individuals who are listed at the end of the appropriate stories. Their generosity to share this information of the area's past with the community greatly helped make this project successful.

I thank Anita Palmquist and Shirley Johnson of the Houston County Historical Society, who have been so helpful in training me as an archivist, and answering my questions on procedure, as well as giving me additional information to supplement the history we have acquired.

I thank Tom van der Linden, editor of the *Houston County News*, who has allowed me to previously share many of these stories in the newspaper, and for allowing me to use them in this book, to share our fascinating history with a larger audience.

Thanks also goes to my editor and publisher, Joel Lovstad, who has formatted the book, created the cover design, given helpful advice and generally seen to all the details of publishing and printing the book.

I especially thank my husband, Len, who proofread and gave me honest advice; my son, Eric, for his technical and moral support; and my son, Ryan, for his moral support in this endeavor. A special thanks to my mother, Marceile Christoph for piquing my interest in history with her scrapbooks of local history of the ghost town where I grew up. I thank my dearly departed father, Herbert Christoph, and my grandmother, Hulda Christoph who inspired me with their stories of the past. A big thank you goes to the rest of my family and friends, especially Betty Christenson, who supported and believed in me. And to God, for answering my prayers.

CONTENTS

INTRODUCTION

I've been creating the archives of the La Crescent Area Historical Society for over 12 years. As I catalog information and artifacts, I frequently come across amusing and interesting information – real stories about the area's real past. When I started the archives in our 3-year old organization in about 1993, I wanted to share these stories with the community to provide awareness of our local historical society and the area's rich history. I asked Tom van der Linden, editor of our local newspaper, if he would print them. Mr. van der Linden was very accommodating, and through the years, many of these stories have been published in the *Houston County News*. I thank Tom for doing that, and for allowing me to publish them again in this book, for a wider audience.

The purpose of this book is meant to be not so much a complete history of the La Crescent area, but rather to share the wonderful, long-forgotten local interest stories, and to entertain as well as inform the reader of Southeastern Minnesota's fascinating past.

It should be stressed that these stories are only as accurate as the information I have found within the archives. Working there, I have come to realize in tracing history that accounts of the same story may vary according to different sources. A history written by one account may not agree with a personal history, especially on exact dates, as often times history is written as remembrances after many years have passed, and the dates get confused. So, the stories in this book are correct according to the available information. Occasionally, a later source turns up information that appears to be more complete, and perhaps more accurate.

I have done extra research on some of the more puzzling stories included here, but most information is from our archives, as I wanted the stories to reflect our collection. I find it endlessly fascinating. I hope you do, too!

Donna Christoph Huegel

Stealing
the
Mississippi
River

CHAPTER 1:
BEFORE THE
WHITE MAN SETTLED

WOOLY MAMMOTHS AND
INDIANS OF LA CRESCENT
History of Pre-Settlement
of the La Crescent, Minnesota Area

A stone-tipped spear whooshed by, missing its mark as the mastodon crashed through the trees, followed by running men from an ancient culture yelling in a forgotten language. Their voices once broke the stillness of the forests in the very bluffs and valleys we now know as the La Crescent area, as they chased and hunted the now extinct animals. These ancient native cultures could not have conceived of the White European settlers who would inhabit and dramatically change their homeland some 12,000 years later. Likewise, we would not know they had been here except for the curious burial mounds they left behind, and other finds beneath layers of earth.

The Ice Age ended around 12,000 years ago. Gigantic glaciers that were 1-½ miles thick extended from the La Crescent area back to Hudson Bay. The glaciers that passed through most of this area for some reason did not come within 50-60 miles of La Crescent and La Crosse. Hence, this region is known as the "driftless" region.

During this time, 15-foot tall mastodons, woolly mammoths, caribou, horses and 6-foot long beaver that weighed 500 lbs. populated the area. A massive jaw of a mastodon is in the collection of the Houston County Historical Society.

There is also evidence of a hunting people living in this area at that time. Spear tips have been found along with the animal bones of these extinct animals by area archaeologists, sometimes under 10 feet of creek beds.

Around 10,000 years ago, many of the above animals became extinct and the ancient peoples hunted buffalo. Spear tips changed shape and style around this period.

About 5,000 years ago nomadic people lived in the area. Then around 2,000 years ago, pottery came into use for the first time, indicating a people who stayed in places longer. These were the Hopewell Culture from southern Ohio and Illinois. They had their own territories, actual villages and even gardens. They were also the first mound builders.

These mounds were burial mounds. They were sort of mausoleums in a bark structure covered with mounds of dirt. The mounds of this period were round or conical in shape. About 30 bodies were buried in these. Some were laid out in the center, while older dead were gathered up into "bundle burials" and placed around the perimeter of the gravesites.

There is evidence of a wide trade area from this period, as "grave offerings" included stone smoking pipes, stone knives about two feet long made from Wyoming flint and obsidian from the Yellowstone area. There were also copper breastplates and silver buttons from the Northeast and pearls from the area of Florida. These were thought to be sacred materials.

For unknown reasons the Hopewell era ended about 1,600 years ago. After the Hopewell, local societies continued to hunt and gather in seasonal rounds, but they constructed smaller mounds lacking exotic artifacts.

There were once about 20,000 mounds in the La Crescent / La Crosse area, but there are less than 150 remaining as most have been plowed over for fields or construction has permanently erased their existence.

In the 1880s and 1890s a man named Theodore Lewis who was an archaeological surveyor, mapped over 10,000 mounds in the area. He found some 80 mounds within the boundaries of La Crescent, indicating it had once been a large ancient village. Many mounds were found in the areas of the current *Subway* sandwich shop at 31 S. Chestnut St., the Kwik Trip at 319 S. 3rd St., and Cindy Gerke & Associates at 318 Walnut St. There were a cross and a bird shaped mound facing south from a later mound building culture found along Pine Creek. None of them remain today. Mounds were also found in Hokah, Dresbach and Dakota and all the way up the Mississippi River to Kellogg, Minnesota.

Around 1,000 years ago the mounds changed shape from round to animal shapes. Often there is nothing found in these mounds, an indication that they had different meaning, perhaps being used as territorial markers or trail markers. The Effigy Mounds near Marquette, Iowa is a prime example of these remaining mounds. There, is found a "marching bears" group of mounds as well as bird mounds from about 800-1,200 A.D.

In 1895 a map was made of mounds in the area. (The La Crescent Area Historical Society and The Mississippi Valley Archaeological Center in La Crosse, Wisconsin have copies of the map.) In 1889 the railroad also came across burial mounds in the area and then again in 1906 as more work was being done on the railroads. In the mounds they found pottery containing crushed clamshells, used by the Oneota Culture of 650-750 years ago.

The Oneota Culture lived off the river in the summer, catching fish, turtles, clams and plant foods, and also hunted deer, elk and bison. They were the area's first farmers, cultivating fields of corn, beans and squash with hoes made of bison shoulder blades. They had migrated down the Mississippi from village complexes on high terraces near Red Wing, Minnesota. For the next two centuries Oneota occupation of the La Crosse / La Crescent area was intensive.

Oneota pottery was found in the area of the *Herberger's* department store at Valley View Mall across the Mississippi River in La Crosse, Wisconsin, as well as bird whistles, made from hollow bird bones. In this area were also found charred corn kernels, cobs, beans and buffalo shoulders, used as hoes.

Indian burial mounds locations marked in 1895, are superimposed over a current map of La Crescent to show where they were. Almost none of the mounds of this area have survived the growth of the city and railroads. [LA CRESCENT AREA HISTORICAL SOCIETY EARLY CULTURES MOUND BUILDERS BY GORDON FAY, 2000]

Ten feet under ground at the Cedar Creek Golf Course in La Crosse, in a layer of black dirt, was found ridged fields of the Oneotas. The soil about the black dirt seemed to have eroded from the bluff above it from 1400 – 1450 A.D. This was only the second time ancient ridge farming had been found in the U.S. The soil was so well preserved that even individual planting spots were found in zigzag patterns to make optimal use of planting space in the rows.

At this site was also found deer jaw sickles, needles, chisels and deer toe arrowheads. The Oneotas lived in the La Crosse and La Crescent areas from about 1300-1600 A.D., just before the French explorers and fur traders came.

Nicolas Perrot came to look for Ioway (Iowa) Indian buffalo hunters and found some around the Houston, Minnesota area. These were thought to actually be Oneotas, but he mistakenly called them Ioways. At the Houston area site were found glass beads, iron and brass buttons, gunflints, musket balls and a Jesuit ring.

During the 1800's there were a number of Indian wars in the area between Sauk and Fox tribes who lived south of the Root River, (which is south of La Crescent) against the Dakota and other Sioux tribes to the north, near La Crescent and Dakota up to Winona. The Root River was a virtual "No Man's Land" in the time of wars.

Following President Thomas Jefferson's acquisition of the land west of the Mississippi River in the Louisiana Purchase of 1803, Nathan Boone (youngest son of Daniel Boone) came to the area to help survey a 40-mile wide strip of land to be a neutral zone between the warring Indian tribes. This zone extended from Shore Acres at La Crescent 40 miles south, and to the southwest as far as Clear Lake, Iowa.

By the 1840's a number of treaties had been made between various Indian tribes and the United States government, moving the Indians out of this region so white settlement could be safer. Peter Cameron then founded La Crescent in 1851.

Looking at the area these days, we tend to think of its history going back to the mid 1800's judging by buildings and other things constructed by the white settlers. Yet people have lived in this area a very long time. They left only their dead and remnants of their cultures buried beneath in the earth.

(Sources: Speeches to the La Crescent Area Historical Society by Ernie Boszhardt 1998 of the Mississippi Valley Archaeology Center, La Crosse; and by Dick Walters, Houston County surveyor 1994 and the 1919 *History of Houston County*.)

ROW, ROW, ROW YOUR BOAT
Early Mississippi River Travel

When people think of early river traffic on the

Mississippi, steamboats come to mind. In the heyday of river traffic (1840s -1870s), certainly they were a common sight.

But before these were the birch bark Indian canoes, bateaux (lightweight flat-bottom boats), rafts, keel boats (or barges) and skiffs (long, narrow rowboats) of the explorers, missionaries and traders.

The earliest recorded common Upper Mississippi River travel by white people was transporting mail and supplies to military forts in 1819. Between Fort Snelling in St. Paul and Fort Crawford in Prairie du Chien, keelboats and canoes were used in summer and a sledge drawn over the ice by dogs (referred to as "Canadian ponies") in the winter. This was about 20 to 30 years before La Crescent was settled.

The early traders used Indian canoes, keelboats, bateaux or skiffs.

The canoes were made with a frame of white cedar covered with the bark of a white birch or of "green hides" with the hair to the inside, stretched over a frame of willows. They were 10-20 feet long and capable of carrying two or three tons of cargo. Yet, they were lightweight so they could be easily carried over portages (around places like waterfalls or too shallow water where the canoes couldn't travel). They were paddled with oars and often went 80 to 100 miles a day.

Six or seven men usually rowed the bateaux. They were light-made boats, usually about 40 feet in length, and from ten to twelve feet wide. They could carry about five tons of freight. Two to twenty oarsmen rowed the ordinary skiffs.

Keel boats or barges were pushed by poles stuck in the river bottom with men leaning with their shoulders against the upper end, and shoving the boat along by walking on the deck or on a plank. These barges were at least partially covered with an upper deck for walking upon and as protection for the crew and cargo from the weather. Most also had temporary masts and simple tackle and rigging for use when the wind cooperated in a comparatively straight part of the river channel.

Pushing barges against the current, besides being toilsome and tedious, was unsatisfactory in either high water or low. When the

Excursion steamer "Key City" going north on the Mississippi River, c.1870.
[LA CRESCENT AREA HISTORICAL SOCIETY ARCHIVES]

river was high, poles would not reach the bottom. When water was low, the sandbars "were almost unconquerable obstacles." Yet, in spite of these difficulties, there was considerable river traffic.

The first steamboat on the upper Mississippi was called the *Virginia.* It first passed Houston County in May 1823 on its way to Fort Snelling. This was a big deal at the time, for that had been declared an impossible task due to channel shallowness and obstacles. After that, for nearly 20 years, all the steamboats passing the county were ones chartered by the government to carry supplies to the troops at Fort Snelling.

In 1842, the *Rock River* steamboat was put into general freight and passenger service; and the following year, the *Otter* came. From then on, river travel and trade increased until the railroads were connected to St. Paul and Minneapolis in the 1870s.   Their advent changed the role of the "Mighty Mississippi" forever. Once the Mississippi River had been the Interstate Highway of the day, with many kinds of "vehicles" traveling on it. After the railroads came, the Mississippi became more like a back road for travel and recreation, more like it is today. Now the canoes, bateaux, rafts and skiffs are rarely seen on the Mississippi River, though it is still a mighty river.

Information from the 1919 *History of Houston County*.

CHAPTER 2:
LET THERE BE
LA CRESCENT

THE COLORFUL CAMERONS
The Family of La Crescent's Founder

We used to picture city founders and leaders of countries or even of industry or business to be great people...better and nobler, somehow, than the rest of us. With the news media these days, we find out that some have faults like substance abuse, affairs, and underhanded dealings. Perhaps we'd like to believe that our leaders are the best of mankind. Still, we mostly find they are just human. So we come to Peter Cameron, the founder of La Crescent, and his wife, Emma... who were not only human, but were two of the most colorful characters in La Crescent's history. This story is about Peter and his family.

Peter was born to Mr. & Mrs. Daniel Cameron Sr. of Caledonia, New York around 1802. He was the oldest of a family of three brothers (Daniel, Alexander and Angus) and two sisters (Catherine and Jane). His ancestors originated from Scotland. In his twenties, he headed west by boat from Caledonia, New York to Chicago. There he dabbled in the fur trade and in selling grain for a while until he grew restless, and once again headed west and up the Mississippi River. He stopped at the very young town of La Crosse, Wisconsin in 1843 and established one of the first land claims there near the Mississippi River.

Peter was said to be willful and arrogant and was disliked by many. He married the beautiful Emma Van Sickle in 1845 in La Crosse's first wedding ever. They invited the whole town to the wedding...all 14 people. Peter was the forth of Emma's *ten* husbands.

Peter engaged in the logging and lumber industry, which was just getting started in La Crosse, and which became the early major industry of the city. He had considerable land holdings in both La Crosse and La Crescent. Because of a logging dispute, Peter went to trial for murdering a man in La Crosse in 1849. Myer Katz' *Echoes of Our Past*, a book on La Crosse history states, "Altercations about ownership (of log rafts) were usually settled through the use of firearms. It was not always the man with the rightful cause who emerged victorious."

In the early days of settlement of the area, logs were floated down the Mississippi River during the boom of logging industry from the 1850s until most of the forests of the area were diminished in the later 1800s. [ECLECTIC SCHOOL READINGS STORIES OF COUNTRY LIFE – 1901]

In early July of 1849 a man named "Ellis" was rafting logs down the Mississippi River with another man when the raft broke and logs strayed from them. Peter Cameron was on the river near where Pettibone Park is now, while his wife, Emma, was on the La Crosse shore. They both saw these men scrambling for the logs. Emma hauled a few to shore and called Peter to come.

Although the logs were marked "Ellis" for identification, Emma insisted to Peter that the trees had been illegally cut from Cameron property. How she could tell seems to be a mystery. "Emma, though, was not above such assertions and dealing," according to Mr. Katz.

The raft's men went ashore for supplies in La Crosse, so Peter confronted them about the logs, now himself insisting they were illegally cut from his land. A violent argument ensued and although Peter was ready to take on both men in a fistfight, they turned away.

Peter then sicked his bulldog on Ellis. Ellis freed himself of the dog, but was badly injured. As the man's partner helped him toward the raft, Katz wrote, "Emma came out of her house carrying two rifles. She handed one to Peter and ordered him to shoot Ellis." Peter did, with a shot to Ellis's back. He then approached Ellis and proceeded to beat him on the head to finish him off, alleged the Katz book.

A local merchant, John Levy, witnessed the scene and tried to intervene. But Peter and Emma threatened to do the same to him, reported Katz. So Mr. Levy left and got the help of Dr. Samuel Snaugh (pronounced "Snow") and County Sheriff John Elder.

Peter was arrested and taken into custody. He was chained in the basement of the McSpadden house in La Crosse, which served as the jail at that time.

Ellis was taken by river for medical attention to Prairie du Chien, Wisconsin but he died on the way. He was buried at Brownsville, Minnesota.

Peter Cameron was tried for first-degree murder in Prairie du Chien but was acquitted on grounds of justifiable homicide. It was two years later that Peter Cameron founded La Crescent, in 1851.

[*Note: A more detailed account of the incident can be found in the book, Echoes of Our Past by Myer Katz.*]

While still on the Wisconsin side of the river, Peter named some streets in La Crosse. He owned a plat of land next to that of Thomas Stoddard of La Crosse, so he named the dividing line between the two plats Division Street. Ferry Street got its name from where Peter had planned to establish a ferry at the foot of that street; but he abandoned the project because the bank was too high there.

Cameron Park in La Crosse is named after Peter Cameron. It was in a land tract first owned by Peter that stretched from roughly Pearl Street south to Division Street and from the Mississippi River east to Sixth Street. In 1850, Peter deeded half of this tract to his brother, Daniel, who was 16 years younger; and the other half to prominent land dealers, Dunn and Dousman.

Daniel then returned to his native New York and gave Peter power-of-attorney to handle his La Crosse business affairs, including authority to lay out a public landing, streets, alleys, lots and blocks on his land. Acting on Daniel's behalf, Peter failed to notify the Register of Deeds when he was acting as Daniel's agent in donating some of the land for public use. Subsequently, problems arose with that piece of land.

After founding La Crescent, starting a trading post there and arranging for the platting of a town, Peter also attempted to change the course of the Mississippi River by digging a canal toward the new settlement, in hopes of making it the important river port rather than La Crosse. But that's another story. Peter died at his sawmill in 1855.

As the story goes, following Peter's death in 1855, Daniel went to see Emma about getting some of Peter's vast land holdings around La Crescent. When she refused, Daniel tried to grab a deed from her, at which point she shot one of his fingers off. Daniel then took her to court and was given that property.

Daniel Cameron Jr. built the big house at 435 S. 7th Street in La Crescent with the "widow's walk" on some of Peter's former land for his parents. It was a larger replica of the family home in New York. Daniel Jr. then persuaded his parents to come live there with him. The house has been restored by the current owners and is now on the National Register of Historic Places

Thirty-five years after Peter gave to Daniel the land now known as Cameron Park, Daniel, who was also considered a very shrewd operator, claimed there was a misunderstanding about the intentions of his land's use, saying that he meant the park area to be developed for real estate purposes. Due to haphazard record keeping in those early days of the city, and Emma losing the original plat in a fire in her Iowa home in 1883, Daniel's squabble with the city went on for a decade. When the litigation finally came to an end, the city had to pay the Camerons $6,000 for the land and $10,000 in legal fees.

Angus Cameron, an attorney, came to La Crosse in 1859. Some years later, he was elected to the United States Senate.

There were other Camerons in La Crosse in its early days. They, too, were from Caledonia, N.Y., but not close relatives of Peter. One was Hugh Cameron, who practiced law in La Crosse and became Judge of the County Probate Court. Another was Dr. Dugald Cameron, who owned a great deal of land in the center of the north side of La Crosse. He had a hand in granting names to several La Crosse streets. He named Caledonia Street in commemoration of his native birth city. He also named Avon Street, Rose Street, Cass Street and St. Andrew Street after another town in New York, friends and Scotland's patron saint, respectively. Dugald committed suicide by drowning in the Mississippi River at the end of Pearl Street in 1867.

The Camerons, though important leaders in the history of La Crescent and La Crosse, were just human after all.

Information from *Echoes of Our Past* by Myer Katz and newspaper clippings of undetermined local papers.

STEALING THE MISSISSIPPI RIVER
Peter Cameron's Canal

Peter Cameron was described in the 1919 *History of Houston County* as "…a man of restless energy and vast conception, but had so many different interests that some of them perforce were left uncompleted at the time of his death."

At age 22 Peter started west and paddled all the way from Utica, NY through the Erie Canal, Indiana and Michigan to Chicago via lakes and rivers. There he lived at Chicago Temperance House with a business in fur trading with the Indians. He also cleared land for growing wheat, and had the wheat hauled to Chicago where it was sent to markets in the East.

His fur buying business took him to southern Wisconsin Territory and to the Mississippi River; then eventually to La Crosse. On one of his trips he met Emma Van Sickle who accompanied him and married him.

According to the 1919 *History of Houston County,* "In 1851 Peter crossed the river and built a double log house in section 10, also acquiring 240 acres of land, and 300 acres more along the river. He did what he could to promote the building of a village. In the spring of 1854 he and his brother-in-law, David Richardson, started a store in the Cameron House, putting in several hundred dollars worth of goods. Mr. Richardson attending to the customers."

Peter had given the Gillett (also spelled Gillitt) brothers some land to clear in what is now downtown La Crescent; and they named the spot "Manton". After the land was cleared and they had sold a few lots, Peter realized they had to solve the problem of transportation to lure people to the village.

The history reported: "October 4, 1854 Cameron was granted license by the County Commission to operate a ferry across the Mississippi at his landing near the northern line of the county." Then remembering the Erie Canal, he decided to dig a canal from Target Lake, into which Pine Creek empties, to the Mississippi, diverting the river for easy access to La Crescent.

The book also asserted, "Among other things, it was his ambition to establish a city on the western bank of the river that should rival La Crosse, and even pass it in the race for supremacy, and to that end

The business district of La Crescent in 1898. Peter Cameron's town was slow to settle since it had no natural port on the Mississippi River. [APPLE FESTIVAL BOOKLET – 1955]

he began the construction of a canal from the river to the land available for a site through sections 13 and 14. Though the lake is quite shallow in places, the bottom is soft, and it was thought that the passage of steamers would deepen and preserve a channel." Peter had hoped with his canal to change the flow of the Mississippi River to bypass La Crosse so people would settle in La Crescent instead of La Crosse.

Peter died while erecting a sawmill for his logging business on July 30, 1855. The canal project was abandoned upon Peter's death, estimated just ten weeks from completion.

However, aerial photographs of the area still show the canal Peter Cameron started...and his dreams of what could have been.

Information from the 1919 History of Houston County and an undated newspaper clipping of an unknown local paper.

This photograph is thought to include the notorious Emma Cameron on the right. It was probably taken in McGregor, Iowa 1854 on the occasion of the marriage of her sister, Louisa, on the left to Jacob Klotzbach in the middle. [LA CRESCENT AREA HISTORICAL SOCIETY ARCHIVES]

THE FIERY EMMA WANTED
AN EVEN DOZEN HUSBANDS

Emma Cameron

Emma Cameron was said to be "a woman of unsurpassingly beautiful figure and features..." with her complexion of a delicate olive tint, large black glittering eyes with long, silky lashes, eyebrows "penciled by nature with mathematical precision, arched symmetrically and met above a nose classically accurate and finely nostrilled..." from an unknown writer according to Myer Katz book, *Echoes of Our Past*. It continued, "Her hair was dark, her hands and neck were plump, and kept company to a pair of arching feet put down upon the ground with an emphasis that indicated a precision of character. It is said that such an exquisite piece of womanhood was seldom seen in those early days in the west."

Exact circumstances of her birth aren't known locally, but she was born "somewhere east of the Alleghenies" in 1820, surmised Mr. Katz, and may have been of Pennsylvania Dutch ancestry. Emma claimed her forefathers fought in the Revolutionary War. She moved with her family to Ohio as a child and was promptly disowned by her parents when she married her first husband, a Van Sickle at the age of fourteen.

By the time Emma had met Peter Cameron in his 1840s travels, returning to La Crosse from a fur trading trip to Utica, N.Y., she had already married two other men, a man named Kellogg from the Michigan Territory and Clinton Cunningham. She traveled alone when she met Peter, so he invited her to come along with him. She accepted and spent the rest of her life in the Mid-west.

She married Peter Cameron in La Crosse in 1845, having the first wedding in the still young town. They invited the whole population (14 people) to the wedding. They made their home on 2nd Street, just south of Pearl Street in La Crosse. Emma soon became the leader of society in La Crosse and was known as the "Toast of the Northwest," asserted Mr. Katz.

Emma was a dichotomy, like the Mother Goose nursery rhyme of the "...Little girl with the little curl right in the middle of her forehead. When she was good, she was very, very good, and when she was bad, she was horrid!" According to Katz, "She was often seen galloping up Front Street in La Crosse astride her spirited white horse, holding a rifle across her knees. She was an expert shot and on more than one occasion helped her husband fight off marauding Indians or return the fire of river bandits. She knew several Indian dialects well and established a friendly relationship with them. This once saved Prairie La Crosse from a massacre when she succeeded in talking the Indians out of a planned attack."

When she died in 1905, her eulogizer said, "She was a good woman in her way; warm hearted, she embodied a spirit of kindness and generosity, yet incapable of deep abiding affection. She had her place among the pioneers, and when her day of youth and beauty was past, took up with a stout heart and cheerful spirit the long narrow years of obscurity, labor and poverty," according to Katz.

Still, Emma was most known for her fiery temper and colorful language. Katz tells a story of Peter and Emma picnicking along the shore of the Mississippi River with several other people in August of 1852. Peter was reading a book after the picnic and Emma was happily singing till she wanted to talk with Peter. Peter ignored her repeated calls, and as she grew angry, he got in his skiff and rowed away down the river. Emma subsequently flew into a rage, and stormed home.

A while later, people heard Emma screaming, "Help! Help!" so they ran to her house supposing Peter had come back and was beating her. They found her alone, thrashing about on her bed. A number of men entered and held her down, "for her safety". It was said that men who had been eager to touch the beautiful Emma were holding down nearly every inch of her body.

She may have been faking a seizure just for the attention, but when the men were getting a bit too familiar, she began kicking, clawing, swearing and screaming at them, telling them in no uncertain terms just what she thought of them and men in general, till they fled "like rabbits" from her explosive temper. Peter returned the next day. Emma found him at the river and took him home.

In another instance, at home, Emma was composing a poem and Peter was reading when again, Peter ignored her desire for conversation. Emma grabbed Peter's book and threw it in the fire. Annoyed, Peter gave her a shove and she fell against a cross cut saw that was leaning against the wall, badly cutting her side. She then ran bleeding to the home of Squire John Levy, a prominent pioneer everyone went to with his or her troubles. She urged Levy to get Peter arrested for abusing and attacking her. But knowing Emma, he doubted her story. So, she began to disrobe to show him her injuries. He put a stop to that as his wife was also there, and sent for Dr.

Snaugh for medical attention. The next day Emma packed her belongings and left for an unknown destination for the entire winter. In the spring, Peter went looking for her and brought her back, though the details of where she was or what she was doing were never disclosed.

When Emma returned, she learned that their neighbor lady had done Peter's laundry, cooking and cleaning while she was away. Though it was 10 o'clock at night, Emma's fury drove her to the neighbors, with axe in hand, to break down the door as they were sleeping. She went on a rampage, smashing windows, and swore she would kill the "black dogs" in their beds. The woman grabbed her child and fled with her husband to hide in the night behind scrub oaks. They dared not hide out in their barn as she also threatened to burn their barn down with them in it! She destroyed everything in sight with her axe.

The next day Peter went to these frightened neighbors to make peace and pay for damages. Emma again grabbed her axe and swore she'd chop off all their heads. After considerable effort, Peter calmed her down somewhat and took her home.

Finally, Peter was about to divorce Emma in 1854 for her "eccentricities" with other men, but he died before the divorce was accomplished. Emma remained a widow for nearly four years before marrying Ralph Bowles in June of 1858. It was after this that Peter's brother, Daniel, approached Emma about inheriting some of Peter's vast land holdings in La Crescent. After she shot one of Daniel's fingers off as he tried to grab the papers from her, he had her charged with attempted murder. She claimed self-defense, but lost the case, as Daniel showed Emma didn't divorce her previous husbands before marrying Peter. So, Daniel was given the land he sought in La Crescent.

Mr. Bowles had already left Emma before the scuffle with Daniel Cameron, and never returned to her. He went to Pikes Peak and then on to Missouri, where he killed a soldier. He was thought to also be killed in the brawl. His body was returned to Emma for burial.

Emma next married husband number six, John Sharp from Iowa. That marriage again was short-lived. Husband number seven was another Van Sickle, a brother to her first husband. He had long remembered her exquisite beauty and came to La Crosse as soon as he learned she was once again available. So, they lived at his rich farm at Elkader, Iowa. He died not long after.

Emma's eighth husband was an elderly neighbor of Mr. Van Sickle. His name was Michael Stence. He heard Emma's sweet voice singing one day as he was farming. Searching out the source, he found Emma and was enamored of her great beauty. They wed and soon he, too, died.

In 1892, at the age of 72, Emma walked 75 miles back to La Crosse. She vowed to never marry again. But still very attractive, she consented to marry a Mr. Eastman. Of course, he also died. Finally, Emma married a Mr. Wilson of McGregor, Iowa. Again, he died before Emma.

But near the end of her life Emma Van Sickle, Kellogg, Cunningham, Cameron, Bowles, Sharp, Van Sickle, Stence, Eastman, Wilson said she only regretted that she didn't have an even *dozen* husbands!

Emma is buried along with six of her ten husbands in a small private cemetery on her own land near McGregor, Iowa. Most of the husbands' marble slabs are marked only with the husbands' initials. One grave has no marker at all, and is thought to be that of Ralph Bowles, the only husband who deserted her. Clinton Cunningham's marker reads: "Clinty, my heart sings to thee, love; In heaven I hope to meet above. You was ever kind and true to me; So was I to you. Emma G.V." And Peter's grave says: "Peter, died January 12, 1854, aged 53 years. By Emma". [*Note: The death date Emma put on Peter's tombstone is different than the 1919 History of Houston County date of July 30, 1855. Because of other recorded events, it is likely that the 1855 date is correct, and Emma lost track after many years between the reburial and so many husbands.*] In an obscure corner of the graveyard, a small stone marker is inscribed: "Peter D., son of Peter and Emma Cameron". But people said Emma never had any children and sarcastically called her "Virgin Em." They thought it was just a mock burial to aid in the legal battle against Daniel Cameron for Peter's fortune.

Still, throughout most of her life, Emma referred to herself as Emma Cameron, and Peter remained one of her favorite husbands.

Information from *Echoes of Our Past* by Myer Katz.

A photo of La Crescent and its apple orchards looking southeast from a bluff top on North Ridge (a.k.a Apple Blossom Drive) c. 1940s – 1950s. The orchards eventually moved farther out of town and this area, once known as Old Hickory Orchard, is now filled with new houses. [APPLE FESTIVAL BOOKLET – 1960]

WHAT DO YOU CALL THIS PLACE?
La Crescent's Three Names

Even before Minnesota was a state (1858) there was La Crescent. Actually, in the beginning La Crescent was known as Camerons, after Peter Cameron, the first white settler of this area. An early history of La Crescent is told in a *La Crosse Tribune and Leader Press* from around 1917. The following is the newspaper account as then written:

> The first man to locate on this spot was Peter Cameron, who erected a comfortable log house here in the spring of 1851. The first steps taken toward the location and actual platting of a village was by the Gillett Brothers, Harvey and William, who had taken the northeast quarter of section ten. The Gillett family consisted of these two

young men and two still younger brothers and a sister, with their mother, who was a widow. They had come to La Crosse from Ohio, and having caught the small pox and in some way lost their money, they found themselves in the pest house entirely destitute; but Peter Cameron became interested in the case and through his influence, they went over and took his claim. The young men were unmarried and the claim was entered in their mother's name. The first plat was about forty acres on the southwest of the northeast of section ten. They procured some oxen, and afterwards broke up some land. The place was called Manton and this part of the village [*Note: what is now downtown La Crescent*] still bears the name on the records. They commenced selling lots from the first as the prospect of having a large city grow up here seemed most favorable.

In the fall of the year 1855, Col. Wm. R. Mercer of La Crosse went over and erected a hotel. This was run by him for about two years. Soon after the Colonel came John A. Anderson, from Springfield, OH, who erected a building and put in a stock of general merchandise. Charles Sperry opened a blacksmith shop the same year. Up to the spring of 1856, the Gillett's did good business in disposing of house lots at a good round figure, and when they finally sold out, they were in good circumstances. They moved to La Crosse and then to Hastings.

The Kentucky Land Company came to Manton in 1856, buying the rest of the Gillett's land for land speculation in the West. They built 12 houses in the new town and sold them to settlers. They wanted a more appealing, romantic sounding name for the town to entice buyers to the area for the lots they sold there. So, it was the Kentucky Land Company that came up with the name "La Crescent" for the bend or crescent shape of the Mississippi River flowing around the town. At least, that's one story of its naming.

The Cameron's remained in the community. Although Peter died in 1855, his brother, Daniel, built a house on some of Peter's land. That house still exists at 435 S. 7th St. in La Crescent, and is presently a private home. The current owners restored the house in the 1990s and it is listed in the National Register of Historic Places.

Information from the *1919 History of Houston County*, and current information.

John S. Harris, (c. late 1800s) Minnesota's first apple grower, who became known as "the father of orchardists in Minnesota". He was also a founding member of the Minnesota State Horticultural Society. [LA CRESCENT APPLE FESTIVAL BOOKLET – 1958]

YOU CAN'T GROW APPLES IN MINNESOTA

John S. Harris

John S. Harris was one of the early settlers of La Crescent and early on, was responsible for giving the town its identity as the "Apple Capitol of Minnesota," a title the city copyrighted in 2002. La Crescent claimed the title not because it necessarily grows the most apples in the state anymore, but because it successfully grew the first apples in a harsh climate where it was thought impossible to grow apples.

There are letters of very early settlers in the Minnesota Territory craving apples. Yet every time someone tried to grow apple trees, the trees were killed out by the severe winters of Minnesota. So, as stated by Minnesota's first apple grower, it was widely believed by "ninety-nine out of a hundred people that you can't grow apples in Minnesota!"

But that was before John S. Harris came to La Crescent. His was a true American success story. John Samuel Harris was born in Seville, Medina County, Ohio on August 17, 1826. His ancestors were among the "founders and defenders of the republic." His parents, Samuel Harris of Connecticut and Mabel Gibbs of Massachusetts, were hardy pioneers who settled in northern Ohio. His father was a farmer, pomologist (fruit grower) and gardener.

At a very young age, John exhibited a great love for horticulture, learning from his father and whatever scarce books he could find on the subject. When he was just eleven years old he started and managed his first nursery and garden. He farmed with his family until his father's death in 1844. Upon the advice of his guardian, he then served an apprenticeship as a cabinetmaker.

In the spring of 1847, Harris enlisted as a private in Company H, 15th U.S. Infantry to serve in the war with Mexico. With his regiment, he joined General Scott at Pueblo and was in the campaign that resulted in the capture of Mexico City. Of the 91 men in the Company, he was one of only 26 who returned home alive. Eventually, he was the last survivor of the Company.

After his return from the war, he remained in Ohio for about one year before heading west. He set a home base in Walworth County, Wisconsin, and from there he traveled throughout Wisconsin, northern Illinois and Iowa. His main objective of traveling was to recover his health, which had suffered severely from the hardships of his war experience in Mexico.

In summer 1851, Harris came to La Crosse, Wisconsin, still in poor health and with only one shilling to his name. Later on he wrote about the experience for the Wisconsin Historical Society, giving this account:

> I started on foot from East Troy, Wisconsin, early in the spring of 1851, having with me a good rifle, a well-trained

bull-dog, and carrying a carpet-bag containing a change of clothes. On arriving at the Dells of Wisconsin, I found that a new bridge was being built across the river at the narrowest place, and that the roads, where there were any, were so muddy as to make traveling difficult. So I stopped off at that place and took a job of grading on the bridge approaches to prepare it for crossing with teams. Most of the time I boarded with a Mr. Gates; later, at a hotel at the foot of the Dells.

In the latter part of June, I arranged to accompany a young man by the name of Chapman...[*Note: This was not the already-legendary John Chapman, "Johnny Appleseed", since that Chapman traveled no farther west than Indiana*]...and we started on foot for La Crosse, traveling on an Indian trail, as at that time there was no road thither, and it was reported that but one wagon had ever gone through on the route. We camped out nights, taking no provisions with us but bread, depending for meat upon shooting pigeons and partridges, which were plenty on the divide between the Dells and Sparta. At one point on this divide, the Indian trail branched, and we lost two or three day's time by going in the wrong direction down into the Kickapoo Valley, and had to go back to the point where the trail branched and start again.

When we arrived in Sparta, our provisions were entirely gone, and we could get no breakfast until Mr. Picket, who was erecting the first log house in Sparta, returned from La Crosse with provisions. We learned here that a family named Brown were living three miles north of Sparta on the road to Black River Falls. We thereupon went on, and at this house, about 10:30 in the morning, we partook of a royal breakfast of fried pork, cornbread, and blackstrap molasses.

Next day we struck Black River at Robinson's mills, and finding a raft of lumber was about to be run out and down the Mississippi, I engaged a passage to La Crosse, where I landed on the morning of July 7 or 8, and on that same day began work on the old Black River House, which was being built by W.W. Bennett.

The frame was already raised and the roof on, but the sides were not enclosed, when I arrived. I made the window sash and panel doors for the house by hand, and believe it was the first work of that kind done in La Crosse. As soon as the building was enclosed, I made a number of bedsteads of pine lumber, procured hay to fill the bedticks of a German living out near the foot of the bluffs. I used fine shavings for pillows and Mackinac blankets for bedding. Bennett started up a first-class hotel.

The bar consisted, at first, merely of a barrel of whiskey with a tin cup on top; but a little later two kinds of brandy were added – one genuine cognac, and the other manufactured on the premises out of whiskey and burnt sugar. Bennett would not let a drunken man drink on the premises, and would not sell drinks on Sunday; neither would he receive paper money in payment for drinks or hotel bills. Only gold or silver was current with him. He would take copper pennies in change, but to get rid of them would go out and heave them into the river. If the river should ever go dry, a considerable mine of copper would be found in front of Spence's drug store.

About this time, La Crosse and other upper Mississippi points were having a boom. The steamboats War Eagle and Menomonie were crowded with home seekers and businessmen looking for places to better their fortunes.

These boats generally arrived at La Crosse about midnight, when a number of passengers were sure to stop off. Hotel facilities were so limited that Bennett managed on the nights of the boats' arrivals to have all beds vacated as soon as the approaching boat whistle was heard, ready to be filled with new arrivals.

For several weeks my business was to oversee the lodging apartment, assist in waiting on table, and add variety in the bill-of-fare. I occasionally went out to the woods that skirted the slough, where the cemetery is now (1901) located, to get a good mess of wild pigeons, which were then very plenty, sometimes changing to a lot of gray squirrels from the bank below to the present Green Bay station, or a string of trout from the Mormon and Chipmunk Coulees. Later in the season, Bennett sold the Black River House to D.C. Evans of Dodgeville, to be used for a store and commenced building the old New England House upon which I also worked.

December 24, 1851, I was married to Miss M.J. Clayton of Montgomery County New York, at the residence of B.B. Healy, Rev. W. Card officiating. [*Note: Harris had met his bride, Melissa, at the boarding house where he was staying. This was only the second wedding performed in the still-young La Crosse.*]

Soon after, we began housekeeping in a small building near McDowell's new boarding house between Third and Fourth Streets, near Vine; and were living there at the time of the murder by William Watts of David Darst, in the Mormon Coulee. I was appointed a special deputy sheriff under Sheriff Eldred to summon a coroner's jury, and procured a team and got started a little before midnight on Saturday night.

We arrived at the scene of the murder just as it began to break day on Sunday, and found Darst's body in a clump of bushes several rods from the house, which was stripped of everything except an axe-helve which was supposed to have been used by the murderer in committing the deed. As soon as it was fully daylight an inquest was held, at which I believe, a Dr. Johnson was the physician, and we returned to La Crosse with the corpse. I was well acquainted with C.B. Sinclair and his son, W.F. Sinclair, who now resides in Money Creek, Minnesota, and personally know that all of the statements he has made in regard to that first murder case in La Crosse are facts.

A few evenings before the escape of the prisoner, I met a posse of about a dozen men coming down Main Street toward where the prisoner was kept, intent upon taking him out and lynching him. I halted them and, after a long parley, persuaded them to give it up. Afterward I almost regretted having done so, for before he was again captured and tried, hanging was abolished by the laws of the state.

Harris came to La Crescent in 1856, five years after his wedding, with two children in tow and established his Sunny Side Garden orchard at the foot of Apple Blossom Drive. He had tried gardening in La Crosse, but moved across the Mississippi because the soil in La Crosse was too sandy for growing fruit trees. His first year in La Crescent, he grew garden produce and berries to sell. In 1857 he planted his first apple orchard, adding more trees every year on his 40 acres, studying and experimenting with them until he developed apple trees hardy enough to withstand the climate despite the claims that "you can't grow apples in Minnesota".

He began displaying his fruit, at Minnesota state fairs, marveling fair-goers and winning nearly every prize in horticulture. His fame grew, and he became an authority on horticulture for this type of climate. The Minnesota State Horticultural Society, which he helped organize and in which he held a variety of offices for over 20 years, "became one of the most forceful of its kind" according to an area news clipping.

John S. Harris also was elected to the State Agricultural Society and assisted in securing the first state aid for "Farmer's Institutes". Later, almost every state appropriated money for the support of agricultural schools. He was founder of the Minnesota Fruit Growers Association and special agent of the division of pomology for the U.S. Department of Agriculture. He displayed a pomological exhibit at the 1883 World's Fair in Chicago and became a manager with the State Board of Fairs of Minnesota, who also promoted the exhibition of flowers at fairs and awarding premiums and prizes for the best. John S. Harris became a "household name throughout the Northwest" in his day and was known throughout the country as a distinguished horticulturist.

He also served as superintendent of the La Crescent Presbyterian Church Sunday school for 12 years. Mr. Harris lived the rest of his 74 years in La Crescent and died in 1901 after an illness lasting several weeks. Upon his death, a 1901 *St. Paul Pioneer Press* noted, "His name well deserves a place not merely on some musty 'roll of benefactors', but on some more conspicuous and enduring memorial."

John S. Harris was a meticulous and arduous horticultural scientist, who was a much-loved and honored gentleman. He became known as the "Godfather of the Minnesota Horticultural Society". On August 17, 1994 – the anniversary of the birth of Harris – the La Crescent Area Historical Society dedicated that "enduring memorial" near his beloved experimental orchard, Sunny Side Garden, where a city park was named after him. The John S. Harris Memorial Park is located on North Elm Street in La Crescent and features a marker encasing his picture and a brief history of his life.

Information from *Many a Grove and Orchard – The Story of John S. Harris* by Donna Huegel

NEVER SAY NEVER
Sunny Side Garden Experiment Station

People often think just one person can't make a difference. But La Crescent's John S. Harris did, not just to La Crescent, or even Minnesota, but also to the whole world, as he developed apple and other fruit trees that could withstand severely cold climates.

A horticulturalist and pomologist, Harris moved to a very young La Crescent in 1856 with his wife Melissa and the first two of their four children (Emma, Frank, Eugene and Ida May). He started a general gardening, fruit growing and florist business, which he called "Sunny Side Garden". It was 40 acres in the area known as "the Vail property located just east of West Avenue in the vicinity of the old home of Deacon Smith, in a locality known as the Baptist colony". [*Note: In present-day La Crescent, it's the area at the foot of Apple Blossom Drive, to the north and west of John S. Harris Memorial Park, in a section of new houses.*]

In 1857 Harris planted his first orchard and continued planting more trees every year making his place virtually a Minnesota horticultural experiment station. He planted for trial, every choice American variety of apple tree he could get, as well as pear, plum and cherry trees, grapes and other small fruits. So, when John S. Harris planted orchards of apple trees in La Crescent, people were skeptical since it was widely thought apple trees could not grow in Minnesota.

Mr. Harris did, however, have his trials and setbacks. He planted thousands of trees and hundreds of varieties, "a full half of which" he said, "were complete and total failures!" He was nearly wiped out twice, in the winters of 1872-73 and 1884-85, by harsh weather conditions, but he didn't give up.

He used the experience of others' failures with apple trees and observed that they must be acclimatized, like people. He had the idea that if the first or second generations fell victim to the climate, the third may become immune. So he planted the foreign trees and planted the seeds of the apples they bore before succumbing to the rigor of Minnesota winters. When the trees from *these* seeds bore fruit, he selected the best seedlings and from their apples, planting again and again. He persisted and finally shocked Minnesotans with his *Minnesota* apples.

By 1866 Harris was invited to be a founding member of the Minnesota Horticultural Society with his name being first on the roll, after he surprised the other pioneers with the largest exhibit of homegrown fruit that had ever been made for the state fair in Rochester, Minnesota in 1866. The Society was inspired by his success and it became world famous and widely respected for its information on reliable methods of successful horticulture. (The Minnesota Horticultural Society is still going strong with a current membership of over 16,000.)

He told the Society, "Previous to 1865, the fruits of the state were chiefly wild crabs, wild plums, wild grapes, strawberries, blueberries and cranberries, and many of these were found only in certain localities of limited extent. A great many trees of apple, plum and cherry had been planted previously but they met with such speedy and certain death during the following winters that it came to be believed by about ninety-nine of every hundred that it was useless to attempt to raise fruit in such a cold country. The farmers settled back upon this opinion, and claimed that our natural fruits must suffice them until they could make a little with which to locate in some better country."

"The first settlers generally commenced planting fruit trees as soon as they could get a piece of ground broken up, and they usually selected those varieties that were favorites in their former homes, and practiced the methods of cultivation and pruning that were in use in the older states. They had no idea that one variety was hardier than another, and therefore planted largely of the early harvest,

Rhode island greening, golden pippin, jiniton, Rambo, etc., from the Rochester, New York Nursery. These trees planted in the virgin soil made a rank, watery and late growth and seldom survived the second winter. They replanted with western grown trees and fared no better, and very soon it became the universal opinion that apples could not be raised in Minnesota."

Harris credited part of his success with growing fruit, especially apples, to the soil itself. In a report to the Minnesota State Horticultural Society in 1885, he said, "There is not a county within our state better adapted to the raising of most varieties of fruit than Houston County. The soil is the very best, clay and sandy loam prepondering nearly everywhere. There are no extensive tracts of prairie, and the uneven surface of the land furnishes ample drainage and every desirable aspect for protection."

Harris persisted in making La Crescent the home of Minnesota's first apples and gaining the title of "Father of Orchardists in Minnesota". In a place where it was thought impossible to grow apples, Harris once commented about his orchards in the same area, "Some of my trees hang full of fruit till they are ready to break down."

His goal was to provide and promote good fruit stock that would thrive in the harsh climate. He was not interested in financial gain for himself. His willingness to give to others was exemplified by his continual generosity in giving away apples to the many people who frequented his orchards. He found that people ate the apples and saved the seeds to take with them apparently for later planting.

In the 1896 *Annual Report of the Minnesota Horticultural Society* members who made visits to each of the orchards said of Harris' Sunny Side Garden: "We arrived at the home of 'our' Mr. Harris, of La Crescent, late in the evening of August 7th. We were expecting to spend the early morning hours of the next day in looking over his grounds, which are, perhaps, the most interesting of any experimental grounds in the state, but a heavy shower began very

John S. Harris sits on the porch of his home with his grandson, Ralph Harris c. 1897 at his Sunny Side Garden experimental station in La Crescent. The house was torn down in the 1990s to make way for new houses. A sign now marks the site of Sunny Side Garden at the foot of Apple Blossom Drive at the bottom of the bluff (north Elm Street) in northern La Crescent. [LA CRESCENT AREA HISTORICAL SOCIETY ARCHIVES]

soon after daylight and our opportunity of doing any valuable work at this place was about spoiled. The orchard here is situated on the lower slope of the bluff, which rises to the height of several hundred feet. The orchard and vineyard form a semicircle, enclosing fruit and market garden of several acres. This arrangement taken in connection with the view of the river and the city of La Crosse in the distance, makes a highly artistic and beautiful home for this pioneer of Western horticulture..." The report mentioned several varieties of pear and plum trees as well as apple trees, and continued, "...We ought not to omit a notice of some of the fine ornamental and nut bearing trees which adorn the place. Both the sweet chestnut and shellbark hickory were in bearing, and several most perfect trees of white and Norway spruce were standing at least forty feet high. The location of this orchard appears to be quite favorable, and Mr. Harris is encouraged to start a new plantation still higher up the bluff."

In Harris' report from his Experiment Station that year, he stated: "Most varieties of fruits turned out better than I anticipated at the time of making my mid-summer report, although the season has not by any means been the most favorable one. The rainfall with us was very much less than the average, and we had more than the usual number of days of extreme heat." He proceeded to report on his crops of raspberries, an extraordinary crop of currants, plumbs, grapes, and then apples, noting, "About 150 varieties were planted this year, but as small trees suffered more from the May frost than larger ones a great many of the varieties did not mature more than from one or two of the half dozen specimens per tree, and some of those showed frost marks."

His report continued: "In the orchard grounds set apart expressly for the experiment station, about 50 trees were planted in 1890, 50 in 1891, 60 in 1892, 30 in 1893, 30 in 1894, 130 in 1895, making a total of 350. Of this number not a single tree has been injured by sunscald. Trees that failed to live have been re-set with same varieties." (Only a few on average died during this time.) Harris was indeed a busy man, as he also planted hundreds of strawberry plants, plums, raspberries, cherries and pear trees.

He concluded, "Some things we think we are learning. First. That a home grown tree or plant or one from a near-by nursery that is carefully dug with plenty of roots and set at once is worth as much to the planter as a half dozen grown a long distance away, dug, boxed or bundled and exposed in transit and delivery, and that but very few men will make a success of fruit growing as long as they continue to purchase from agents of unknown nursery firms or from foreign nurseries long distances away, instead of raising their own stock or securing it of reliable local nurserymen. Second. That too close planting of trees is not advisable in a climate subject to frequent drouths [*Note: This is Harris' spelling of droughts*]. Third. That the very general failure of the strawberry crop this season is a result of the long drouth that prevailed last season." – June 19, 1896.

By 1895, there were orchards in 17 other Minnesota towns besides La Crescent, as far north as Duluth.

Harris won nearly all the prizes for apples at the first Minnesota State Fair and continued exhibiting them and winning prizes for them until his death in 1901. His well-earned reputation was of a man who never gave up. He was full of hope and when one kind of fruit or method failed, he was ready to try another, proving persistence pays off. He was a man who made a difference because he didn't believe something was impossible.

Information from *Many a Grove and Orchard – The Story of John S. Harris* by Donna Huegel

HOW'D YOU LIKE TO BUY SOME SWAMP LAND IN MINNESOTA?

The Kentucky Land Company

La Crescent owes much to the *Kentucky Company* (also known as the *Kentucky Land Company*) for its early years, although the speculation company was a bit unscrupulous at times. They gave La Crescent its current name, platted much of the city, built the first causeway (the ferry road), ran a ferry before there was a bridge, built a single and double store in the town, and built 12 Kentucky homes in the new city.

The *Kentucky Company* entered into the picture in the development of La Crescent in 1856, when they bought the land holdings that Peter Cameron gave to the Gillett brothers to plat a town. Cameron had founded the town in 1851, and called it "Cameron's". He had met the Gillett family who were down on their luck in La Crosse, and gave them some of his newest land holdings in this area to clear and plat a town. When the Gillett brothers had done this, they re-named the town "Manton," a name that appears on maps of the city's downtown to this day.

The *Kentucky Company* was organized in the spring of 1856 at Louisville, Kentucky. The principal original members were Jared Boyle, J.M. Bryant, Charles S. Waller, Thomas McRoberts and E. Randolph Smith.

The object of the company was to establish a city in the upper Mississippi valley during a time of land speculation in the settlement of the West in hopes of gaining large profits. The *Kentucky Company* was backed by prominent men of the time including George D. Prentiss of the *Louisville Courier*, Will Bross of the *Chicago Tribune*, General John C. Breckenridge and others who purchased lots and were enthusiastic about the scheme.

In June of 1856 the principal stockholders visited the site of their new village. At a meeting held at the Tremont House in La Crosse these stockholders decided upon the present name of La Crescent after the crescent shape of the Mississippi River around the town site. They thought this was a more romantic sounding name than Manton, which would perhaps draw more settlers to the area.

After this meeting, Thomas McRoberts remained in La Crescent as active agent and began selling lots from $250 to $600 each, except for corner lots that they reserved for future use. The spirit of speculation was so intense that an offer of $1,100 for land owned by a non-resident was refused.

One of the 12 original houses built in La Crescent by the Kentucky Land Company in the early days of settlement (1850s). This house sat at 333 south 2nd Street between Walnut and Oak Streets in La Crescent. It was the former residence of the Anton Bahr family. The house was demolished c. 1991 to make way for a senior citizen residential facility named Kentucky Place in memory of the Kentucky Company house it replaced. The place is now known as Claddagh House – Assisted Living for Seniors. [LA CRESCENT AREA HISTORICAL SOCIETY ARCHIVES - COURTESY OF MILO SHEPARDSON]

The town was platted during the winter when the area was snow covered and frozen. So whether the speculators knew it or not, much of the new town was platted on what seemed on paper to be prime bottom land, but in reality was unlivable swamp between the Mississippi River and the present town of La Crescent. Some poor unsuspecting settlers bought lots before coming West only to find when they arrived any time other than winter, that their lots were parcels of Mississippi backwater and swamps.

Thomas McRoberts was also the man who won a charter from the Minnesota legislature for exclusive privilege of operating ferries across the Mississippi in the immediate area of La Crescent. He then charged exorbitant prices for the service until the people were in an uproar about it. They started their own ferry service until McRoberts brought a lawsuit against them and won. He then lowered his prices to a more affordable rate, however.

The double store building built by the *Kentucky Company* in 1857 was at 309 Main Street. Throughout the years it served as a store, newspaper office and print shop, church, school, lodge room, residence and store house. The 12 Kentucky homes, all built to the same architectural design, were scattered throughout the village of La Crescent to make the town seem larger. What Kentucky houses remain have been remodeled and changed almost past recognition as "Company" houses.

The Kentucky Place senior residence at 333 S. 2nd was so-named in the 1990s because it stands on the site of one of the original Kentucky homes. It is now known as Claddagh House, assisted living for seniors. Good and bad, the *Kentucky Company* had a large influence on the early days of La Crescent.

Information from the 1919 *History of Houston County*.

THE POWER OF A LITTLE CREEK

Pine Creek Mills

Although La Crescent is on the bank of the mighty Mississippi River, it was humble Pine Creek west of La Crescent that was harnessed in the early days of settlement for industry. From the 1850s into the 1870s various spots on the creek were used to run saw mills, flourmills and even woolen mills.

The Pine Creek Settlement began in 1852, a year after Peter Cameron founded La Crescent. Technically, these first settlers were "squatters" since land in Houston County was not available for purchase until the Indian treaties were settled in 1854. Then the original settlers were able to purchase the land they were living on by the provision of "Eminent Domain." Among the early immigrants were people of Norwegian, German, Dutch and Irish heritage who were mainly farmers.

The first mill built on Pine Creek was a sawmill started in 1856 by Groff & Co. The mill was 18 by 44 feet and two stories high, with a vertical saw propelled by a turbine wheel run by power from the dammed-up stream. According to the 1919 *History of Houston County*, "It was completed and put into operation May 13, 1857, and developed a capacity of 1,000 feet of lumber a day. It was kept in more or less regular operation until about 1872, when it was sold to T. Casper. The building itself went to Hokah Township, and the machinery beyond St. Cloud. The power was subsequently used by Groff & Co. to drive their flouring mill."

"The Linganore flouring mill" it stated, "was built in 1859 not far from the old saw mill. As originally constructed it was 30 by 40 feet in ground dimensions, with an attic above the second story. It had at first a single run of stones turned by a reaction wheel made by the owners of the mill, Groff & Co."

The history continued, "The Burton sawmill was constructed in 1857...by D. Burton, and was furnished with two sash saws and had plenty of water from Pine Creek. At times it had too much and was finally almost destroyed. An attempt was made to move it to a more favorable location eighty rods down the stream," but business setbacks caused too much of a financial strain for Mr. Burton and the project was abandoned.

"About the time that the Burton mill was erected, another saw mill was put up by Samuel Michael on a branch of the creek...It had a single saw set in motion by an overshot wheel. This mill also was frequently damaged by freshets, [*Note: sudden overflowing of a stream*] and almost as frequently changed hands, each new proprietor hoping for better luck than his predecessor; but in 1866 a greater flood than usual put it completely out of business."

"The La Crescent flouring mill was built early in the (1870s) by D.J. Cameron on his farm...on Pine Creek. It was a two-story frame building, with four run of stones. A dam was constructed to secure a head of seven feet, but it was discovered that in order to maintain that amount the water was backed up to the race [*Note: channel for a current of water*] of the Toledo mill, and after a legal contest it was decided that the dam must be lowered two feet. The project was then abandoned."

"The Toledo Woolen Mills started in 1865 when Thomas Fletcher and J. and N. Webster erected on Pine Creek...a fine stone structure, three stories high, with a good basement, for the manufacture of yarns, flannels, blankets and kerseymeres [*Note: a fine, twilled woolen cloth*]. The machinery cost about $8,000, and included one set of cards [*Note: to separate wool and other fibers into yarns and threads*] 48 inches in width, six looms [*Note: to weave the yarns into material*], a jack [*Note: device for turning or lifting*] with 264 spindles, with sheering [*Note: cutting machines*], fulling [*Note: machines to clean, shrink, and thicken cloth with moisture, heat and pressure*], and other appliances. In 1878 N. Webster bought out Mr. Fletcher and his brother and became the sole proprietor. The local trade was supplied in a retail way, and three men with teams were kept on the road to dispose of the goods manufactured."

Finally, the history added, "In 1860 C.J. Laugenbach put up a flouring mill, with two run of stone, near where the woolen mill was subsequently erected. It did good work until the fall of 1864, when it was destroyed by fire and the woolen mill occupied the power."

An 1878 plat map of the La Crescent area of Houston County denotes the location of these mills. The map and other information may be found at the La Crescent Area Historical Society archives.

Although the Mississippi River was the highway of its day in the area, even small creeks helped bring civilization to the new land.

Information from the 1919 *History of Houston County*.

GO WEST YOUNG MAN
Lorette House Stagecoach Stop

In the early days of Houston County settlement, an important territorial road passed through La Crescent from La Crosse to St. Paul. The first stagecoach stop west after La Crosse was the Lorette House, (also spelled Loretta) on the ridge eight miles west of La Crescent, following what is now County Hwy. 25. (Stagecoach roads through the area in those days followed the ridges rather than the valleys to diminish the threat of Indian ambushes, which were an occasional threat as the white man came into the Indian lands here in the 1850s and 1860s.)

According to the 1919 *History of Houston County*, "The Lorette House was a well known landmark in the early days...It was constructed by Seth Lore (before 1856 – exact date unknown) and kept by him until 1861. After that his daughter, Mrs. C. B. Carpenter, became the hostess."

The Lorette House was a two-story log structure, 18 by 20 feet, with two huge chimneys. An immense fireplace extended along one-half of the side of the inn. The main lodge housed three sleeping rooms on the first floor and a chamber above. There was an extension to the back of the building as a cook room. In 1859 a two-story frame addition of 20 x 30 feet was added. A blacksmith shop, livery barn and other buildings were included in the complex, as stagecoaches drawn by four or six horses changed teams there.

Passengers unloaded at this stop for three different stage lines. The history stated, "...not unfrequently seventy people would be accommodated with dinners..." Another article about the Lorette House said, "Sometimes the Lorette House served nearly one hundred persons at a single dinner." The next stop was eight miles farther at Cooper's Tavern in what is now called Ridgeway.

The history continued, "In 1856 a post office was located at the Lorette House, and E.S. Lore held the postal keys. Mrs. Anna M. Price, a sister of the postmaster, was appointed deputy in the following spring and had charge until it was discontinued, except a single year, when David Davis was postmaster. In 1869 both these offices were discontinued, and the Mound Prairie office established, with J. A. Eberhard in charge."

A drawing of the once busy Lorette House stagecoach stop on South Ridge, west of La Crescent on County Highway 25. The inn is long gone and a farm place now sits where it stood. [LA CRESCENT AREA HISTORICAL SOCIETY ARCHIVES - FROM AN 1871 HOUSTON COUNTY MAP BY BLISS & MARTI]

During the Sioux Uprising (1862) a family named Lore ran the inn. They were Southern sympathizers during the Civil War. A story of their loyalties was told that one day a group of Union soldiers came through. Mrs. Lore, afraid of them, sent her young son to talk to them. The child offered that his family members were Southern sympathizers. To this, one of the soldiers replied, "Say you're a Yankee or I'll run you through!" Out of fear, the boy complied.

A school was also established on one half acre of land donated by Mrs. Anna M. Carpenter of the Lorette House on Sept. 7, 1876. The first meeting was held at the Lorette House. According to the 1882 *History of Houston County*, "It is a neat white frame house, 18 x 30 feet, with green blinds, furnished with plain desk; fine teacher's desk and chair; portable blackboard; full set of the largest size Camp's outline maps and Holbrooks 12 inch globe."

The Lorette House no longer stands and the only known part of it is its sign at the Houston County Historical Society. A farm now sits on the site at a T-intersection. If you go looking for it, you'll know you're close when you see the Lorette Cemetery, which was located south of the inn with land donated by the Lorette House when the need arose.

A large pine tree dominates the cemetery, which was planted there around one hundred fifty years ago to mark the first grave – one of an infant who died along the stagecoach route. It was the only way the young grieving parents had of marking the spot where they laid their beloved baby to rest before continuing on their journey.

Information from the 1882 *History of Houston County*, 1919 *History of Houston County*, undated news article and a speech by Anita Palmquist, area historian of the Houston Country Historical Society.

A PLACE TO REST YOUR WEARY HEAD
La Crescent Hotels

Although La Crescent has yet to grow into a large city, it has almost since its beginnings had places for travelers to rest.

Only four years after Peter Cameron founded La Crescent, Col. Wm. H. Mercer of La Crosse built the first hotel in La Crescent in the fall of 1855. The building was two stories high and was erected on Main Street (then known as "Mississippi Street") just east of the present Telephone Co. building. Col. Mercer ran the hotel for only about two years.

When the La Crescent Female Seminary opened in 1861, the hotel was used as its boarding house. Later, it served as the school, as well. When the proprietors and teachers left for better opportunities elsewhere, the seminary became the La Crescent Hotel once again.

The building was dubbed the "Bee Hive" for a while, and was torn down along with part of the hill it sat upon, to make way for the service drive from Main Street to the new highway when it went through in the 1950's.

In 1871, J.O. Sawyer opened his hotel, known as the Sawyer House, which literally was a house, located on Main and Elm Streets. He sold it to a Mr. Rollins, which began a succession of proprietors. They were Mr. Lafayette Whitehouse, E.B. Webster, and again, Mr. Whitehouse. These men also called their establishment the La Crescent Hotel, as the old La Crescent Hotel was out of business by then. This hotel closed following the death of Mr. Whitehouse, leaving no hotel accommodations in the city for a period of time.

A Mr. McGee put up a third hotel about 1892. This building was located at the southwest corner of Walnut and Main Streets. When the sidewalks were put in about 1912, considerable remodeling had to be done to the structure, since part of the building had protruded out to where the sidewalk was to go. In the middle 1950s, Carl Bahr owned this hotel. It was torn down and the site is currently the *Quillin's IGA* parking lot.

La Crescent's first hotel from the 1850s saw lots of history as it was also used as a "Female Seminary" for a time, was the scene of a bizarre holiday suicide and in its later days was known as the "Bee Hive". It was just east of the Telephone Company building in La Crescent, near the present Post Office. It was torn down prior to the 1950s to make way for Highway 61 improvement. [APPLE FESTIVAL BOOKLET – 1958]

Other motels that came and then disappeared since were: The Minnesota Cabins, the Crescent Motel and the Monte Carlo.

The Crescent Motel was on the northwest corner of N. 4th and Chestnut, the place currently occupied by *Kwik Trip*. A Mr. Ehler had built it perhaps in the 1930s. Bill Vetter also owned it.

The Monte Carlo Motel was also built around the early 1930s by Brownie Beck, who was known for the calliope he pulled with his miniature mules in parades. It was located left of the dock on Sportsman Landing on Shore Acres. It had a bit of a reputation during WWII as a safe haven for "Ladies of the Evening". The Monte Carlo was sold to Roy Enge. His son later owned it until the 1970s.

The Minnesota Cabins were built and owned by Kenneth F. Shepardson, who was also an artist and created the first King Apple for Applefest. These 21 cabins were built about 1945 from government grain bins from Wabasha, Minnesota, since building materials were scarce due to a housing boom following WWII.

These cabins were 12 feet by 16 feet and rented for only $6.00 to $7.00 per night, although they had no separate indoor plumbing. In the early 1950s, they were sold to Sylvester Roth. Roth eventually sold them for the construction of a Mobil gas station. They were at the site of the former "Pump and Munch" gas station, on the northwest corner of South 3rd and Walnut Streets.

The Ranch Motel opened in 1949 under the ownership of A. Sr. and Deborah Moore, and later was owned by Larry and Colleen Collins. It is the sole survivor of La Crescent's hotel business, and is currently under the ownership of Kevin Collins and is now the only public place to rest in La Crescent.

Information from 1958 Applefest Booklet & interview with Milo Shepardson.

A horse pulls passengers in a wagon on a trail going north along the Mississippi River from La Crescent c. 1870s before a road was built that eventually became Highway 61. [LA CRESCENT AREA HISTORICAL SOCIETY ARCHIVES]

YOU CAN'T GET THERE FROM HERE

La Crescent Street Names in 1878

Plat maps of La Crescent and the area from 1878 show a town and countryside much different than today. For one thing, the numbered east-west streets we know as N. 1st or S. 1st, etc, were avenues named after states.

Main St. was known as Mississippi Ave; North 1st was Minnesota Ave; No. 2nd was Wisconsin Ave; N. 3rd was Oregon Ave. The streets south of Main St. in order were: Kentucky, Utah, Iowa, Kansas, Ohio, Illinois, Michigan, Vermont, Indiana, Massachusetts and New York Avenues.

For some reason, parts of the streets in the area of the present La Crosse McCormick building (formerly, the roller skating rink)

This map of La Crescent from 1878 shows street names that no longer exist in La Crescent. The area between the railroad tracks and the Mississippi River was platted in the winter. Come spring most of that area proved to be swamp and Mississippi backwaters where nothing could be built.

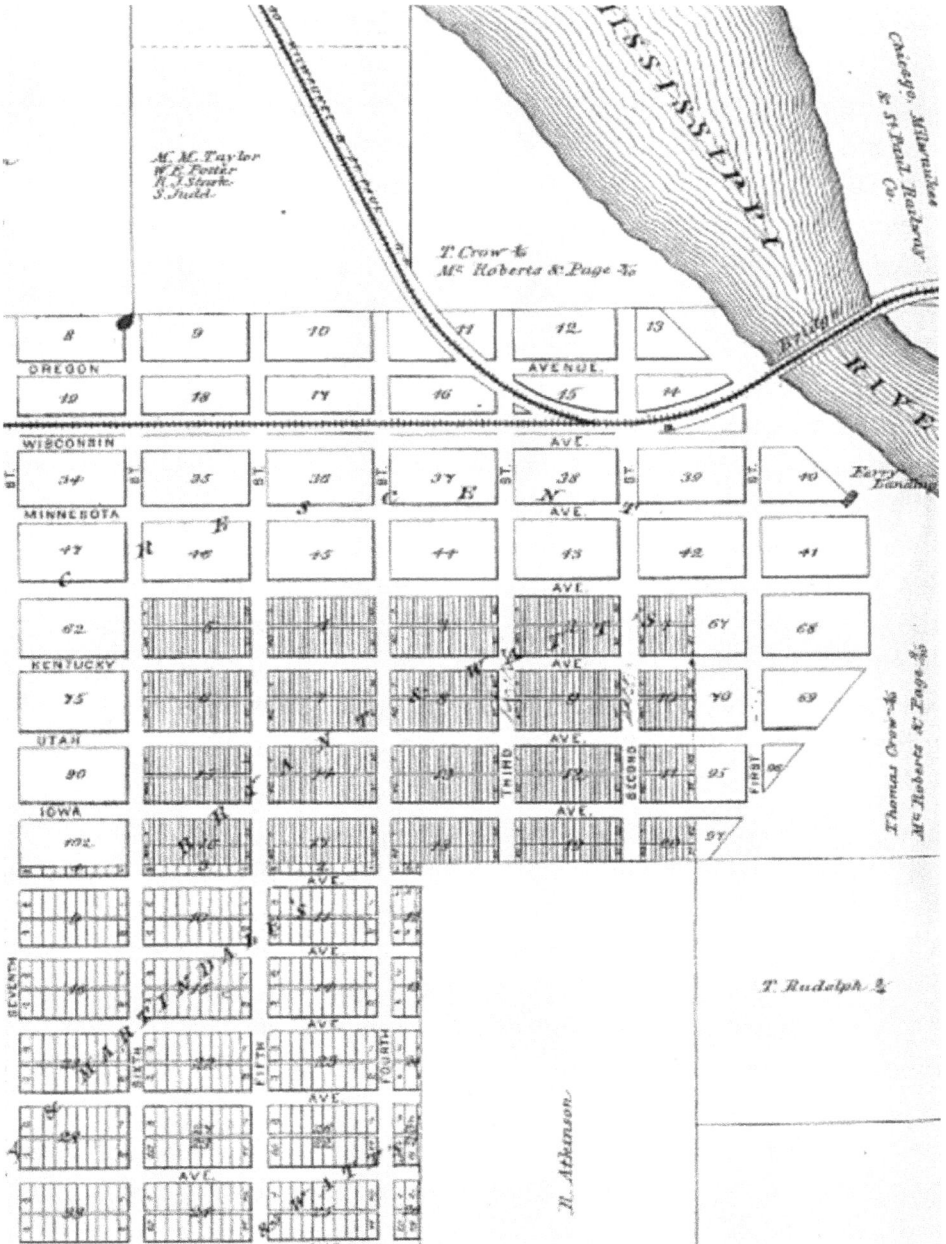

The Kentucky Land Company sold lots there anyway. Note the railroad swing bridge across the Mississippi River. It was built c.1876 and has been in continuous use ever since! [LA CRESCENT AREA HISTORICAL SOCIETY ARCHIVES]

were shown with other names as well for two blocks. Part of Ohio Ave. was Mechanical Ave; part of Illinois Ave. was Agricultural Ave; part of Michigan Ave. was Commercial Ave; Vermont was also Artisan Ave; Indiana was also Crocker Ave. and Massachusetts shared Oneida Ave.

The north-south streets (some of which don't exist today because they were platted in areas under backwaters or swamps of the Mississippi River) were numbered streets. First St. was nearest the Mississippi river, and 8th St. near downtown. From there, the streets heading westward were: Sycamore, Chestnut, Walnut, Oak, Elm, Maple and Hill Streets.

The town map shows all three names of La Crescent: Cameron, Manton, and La Crescent, as well as some other land company names. The railroad "Swing Bridge" over the Mississippi River, which was new then, being built in 1875 - 1876, is also shown on the map.

Evidence of the earliest historical figures in La Crescent is seen on the La Crescent Township map. It indicates Cameron's Canal, started by town founder, Peter Cameron, in an effort to bring river travel to La Crescent in 1854. The land of John S. Harris, Minnesota's first apple grower in 1857 at his Sunnyside Garden area, is listed on the map as well.

The township map (not shown) has the River Junction Depot on the north edge of La Crescent, as well as the railroad crossing, which was in the area of Miller's Pond, south of La Crescent along the present Hwy. 16. Along that highway on the way to Hokah, was also shown the Root River Brewery, a school and two cemeteries.

Going north and west out of La Crescent, flour, saw and woolen mills are shown along Pine Creek, as well as other schools and cemeteries.

Besides the cemeteries, and a few street names, the only physical things that remain in place from those maps today are Cameron's Canal, some railroad lines and the 1876 Swing Bridge.

Information from 1878 plat maps donated by Gordon Fay.

LA CRESCENT'S BURIED BUILDINGS
Smith Grubber Buildings

If someone did an archaeological dig in La Crescent, they might find the ruins of a once thriving business in the town. Beneath Highway 16 and 61 just west of the viaduct to La Crosse, lie the buildings of the W. Smith Grubber Company. It started in the late 1890s by William Smith and his sons, Frank and Martin.

The W. Smith Grubber Company building c.1900 is buried under Highway 16-61 at the stoplight near the viaduct in La Crescent. The man in the photo is not identified. [APPLE FESTIVAL BOOKLET – 1958]

The business manufactured stump pullers or "grubbers" for the purpose of clearing new land of trees for farming. The grubbers were a vast improvement over dangerous dynamiting, and were far less work than digging out the stumps with a shovel. The grubbers employed the use of pulleys and ropes pulled by a horse to twist the stump out of the ground.

The business expanded until there were a number of stone buildings. They included an office, warehouse, foundry, pattern room, and storage sheds for scrap iron.

According to an article by Mildred Shanley, written around 1958;

> "...the number of employees increased and the volume of mail helped the local post office. Everything was rosy; then came World War I and exports dropped. After the war the rapid advance of the motor age finished the Grubber Company...the Smith grubbing machine belonged to the horse and buggy era."

The article also stated, "the factory was situated just west of the tracks, under the viaduct. The buildings are still there, buried under a modern highway."

It kind of makes you wonder what else lay hidden and forgotten beneath the ground, doesn't it?

Information from 1958 Applefest booklet.

HEY, DADDIO
La Crescent in the 1950s – 1960s

The La Crescent of the 1950s and '60s was a bit

different than now. Not only were orchards more abundant and located where new houses now sit on streets named after apples, but it also was much more a small town unto itself rather than the commuter community it's becoming for La Crosse.

It was a time when neighbors knew one another well and residents had most everything they needed in their own little town. Schools were being built and an addition was put on the elementary school for the post-war baby boom. It was a simpler time with simple phone numbers like: 11 for Harris Grocery, 66 for the La Crescent Motor Co., 93-W for La Crescent Electric Co., or 14-R-2 for Kletzke Plumbing & Heating.

The La Crescent of 1954 had at least five gas stations (probably with a full service attendant to fill your gas tank, check your oil and the air pressure in you tires, and wash your windshield), two grocery stores, two motels (the Crescent Inn and the Minnesota Motel), a clothing store and three restaurants. Carroll's Restaurant and Bar was the place for La Crescent friends and neighbors to gather for local fun with dancing every Saturday night from 9 p.m. to 1 a.m.

By 1961 there were four motels (with additions of the Ranch Motel and the Panorama Motel), more places to eat with the Commodore Night Club, Niebuhr's Coffee Shop, and following the car trend, the A & W Root Beer Stand and "Bucket" Drive-In, where local teens liked to meet and hang out. There was more entertainment in La Crescent, then, with two bowling alleys (Karroll's, also spelled "Carroll's" and Shamrock Lanes), besides a golf course and driving range.

The following were La Crescent businesses that had ads in the 1954 Apple Festival booklet: La Crescent State Bank, *La Crescent*

Carroll's was a hot spot of activity in La Crescent in the 1940s and 1950s with a restaurant, bar, bowling alley and Saturday night dances. In the 1950s it advertised steaks, fish and liquor; and its phone number was 2. It was along Highway 61 where the Subway sandwich shop is now at 31 S. Chestnut St. [APPLE FESTIVAL BOOKLET – 1958]

Times – Hokah Chief (newspaper), La Crescent Lumber and Coal Co.; Metropolitan Life Ins. Co – Harold D. Dodds, Rep.; La Crescent Motor Co.; J.M. Gittens – Insurance; La Crescent Electric Co.; The Crescent Inn; Dr. L.W. Gittens; Barber Shop – Pete & Don; La Crescent Telephone Co.; Hugh Fay Apple Market; La Crescent Pharmacy; Luther Super Service (Mobile Products); Harris Grocery; Bateman Bros. General Contractor; La Crescent Beauty Shop; A & W Root Beer Drive-In (Hwy 61 – Jim and Agnes, Props.); Rudy's Skelly Service; Minnesota Motel; Niebuhr's Coffee Shop; Bob's I.G.A. Super Market; La Crescent Farm and Orchard Supply Co.; Carroll's; La Crescent Outboard Service; Scanlon Turkey Farm; Mathy Construction Co. general Contractors; Mid-West Motors; Reider's Standard Service ("Everyone Knows Windy") Howard Papenfuss (Standard Oil Products); Skelly Oil Co.; Timm's Toggery (Men's – Women's – Children's Ready-to-wear); Kletzke Plumbing and Heating; Arnoldy's Appliance; Charley Bros. (Metal Fabrication); Clarence's Plumbing, Heating and Air Conditioning (Clarence Vonderohe); La Crescent Brush and Spray (Howard Peart); The Sportsman's Bar (Stan Gittens,

Prop.); Tri-State Erection Co. (Joe Strupp) and Vindal's Hardware.

(Note: none of the businesses used "apple" in their name then.)

Apple orchards flourishing in the North Ridge area were: Fruit Acres (Gordon Yates, mgr.); Old Hickory Orchard (Russell Senn mgr.); Leidel's Orchard (Victor Leidel); Lautz Orchard (Louis Lautz); Little Swiss Fruit Farm (Mrs. Vollenweider and son) and Harris Orchard (Lyle Harris) – a descendant of the first Minnesota apple grower, John S. Harris from 100 years earlier.

South Ridge was also covered with apple orchards by then. They were: Evans Orchard (Kenneth and Mildred Evans, owner/ operator); Burrows Orchard (Carl Burrow); Winsky Bros. Orchard and Kroehler Orchard (Raymond Botcher, mgr.).

Other area apple orchards listed were: Clarence Vetsch Orchard, Hillside Orchard, Webster's Orchard operated by Willard Steinke and Southwind Orchard.

Like most small towns, chances are many small businesses in La Crescent had trouble competing with bigger businesses with perhaps more to offer in nearby La Crosse. With the advent of the automobile age, people could easily travel farther for shopping, entertainment and services, and they did. Local patronage was drawn away from La Crescent until many small businesses that could no longer compete had to close their doors for good. But even as businesses closed and changed, La Crescent still draws people who wish to live in the beauty of the area, and it continues to grow anyway.

Information from 1954 & 1961 Applefest booklets.

DUCK AND COVER...
THE COMMUNISTS MIGHT ATTACK!
La Crescent's Fallout Shelters

Since September 11, 2001, America has had to focus on the matter of security in our country. We now have yellow, orange and red alerts and a new federal office of "Homeland Security" to inform us about likely terrorists' attacks. But it's not the first time America has felt threatened at home.

Other life and world changing events were the development of the nuclear bomb, and its use in World War II. After that, the world became a significantly more perilous place in which to live. The way our country handled the growing threat during the Cold War and following the 1963 Cuban Missile Crises at home, was with the Civil Defense Act of 1950. From the federal level, offices were created regionally, then by state, and down to the local level, where La Crescent comes in.

Following much news and fear mongering, La Crescent, like towns all across the U.S. came up with its own plans for surviving a nuclear attack. At a time when people were instructed how to build their own "fallout shelters", "Communists" were being rounded up in the era of McCarthyism and kids in 1950s schools were taught to "duck and cover" in case of a nuclear attack, La Crescent came up with its own Civil Defense plan in 1959.

The plan called for 26 volunteers who were members of the Police Auxiliary to help guard local designated points of strategic value from any kind of attack. These places included the radar tower for the La Crosse airport on North Ridge and area bridges, which were then watched day and night, around the clock for suspicious activity. A siren was also installed on City Hall to warn of an emergency.

These Civil Defense volunteers also became certified in first aid from the Red Cross in the event of a disaster, learned how to use radiation detection devices to check for unsafe levels of "fallout" following a nuclear attack, and built a model fallout shelter in Veteran's Park, near the American Legion building, according to Don Anderson, who was one of the Civil Defense volunteers from 1959 through 1964.

The model, which was behind the present Crescent Inn, was for area people to see so they could build their own fallout shelters in their basements. The plan suggested space requirements of 10 square feet per person with the shelter having two windowless existing walls. Any windows in the shelter area were to be blocked by sand bags, or filled concrete blocks set on the outside wall. The entrance was to be two feet wide and shielded with at least two right angle turns.

This sample fallout shelter was built at Veteran's Park near La Crescent's American Legion building in 1963. It was torn down in the 1970s. Some of the builders are left to right: Winston Reider, Don Anderson, Ken Sherwood, Bill Atchison, Tony Gartner, Clarence Vetsch and Everett Harlos. [LA CRESCENT AREA HISTORICAL SOCIETY ARCHIVES – COURTESY OF DONALD ANDERSON]

These shelters were to then be equipped with a two-week supply of canned food, a can opener and pocketknife, eating utensils and seven gallons of water per person. Since the people couldn't leave the shelter until it was safe, they were also to provide for sanitation. For this they needed a 20-gallon can, 10 gallon covered pail, toilet paper, towels, grocery bags and newspapers, household chlorine and rubber gloves. Other suggested equipment listed were a battery radio with extra batteries, radiation meters, a flashlight with spare batteries, clothing and blankets, a first aid kit, tools, and things like writing, reading and game supplies to ward off boredom. Items that were to be in reach were cooking equipment and matches, fire fighting equipment and rescue tools in case the shelter occupants had to dig themselves out.

The basements of the elementary school and the Church of the Crucifixion School were designated fallout shelters and were stocked with food, water and medical supplies where members of the community could go for safety during a nuclear attack if they didn't have home shelters. They would then be required to stay there until it was determined by a Civil Defense volunteer that it was safe to go back outside.

The original members of the Civil Defense Auxiliary Police in 1959 were: Donald Anderson, Richard Gasper, Thomas Mueller, William Dumond, Joseph Hodge, Sgt. Nathan Randall, Sgt. Hank Abnet Jr., Frank Wally, William Lathrop Sr., Everett Harlos, Fred Otto, Sec. Laverne Link, Lt. Kenneth Sherwood, William Atchison, Lt. Clarence Vetsch, Capt. Winston Reider, Anthony Gartner, John Zlabek, Donald Buchan, Frank Wolff, Sgt. Arthur Oldenburg, Edward Layland, Sgt. John Kathan, Frank Wally, William Lathrop Jr., and Glen Hove.

Sometime in the 1970s the model fallout shelter in Veterans' Park was torn down and gradually, supplies within the fallout shelters were disposed of. The Civil Defense volunteers mostly spent their time doing more mundane chores like teaching first aid to the

Boy Scouts, riding with Police in their vehicles, helping with security and directing traffic at local events.

The local Civil Defense program, which focused on nuclear attack, dissolved over the years and became instead, a department of Emergency Services prepared for any disaster, and having a similar hierarchy. According to La Crescent Police Chief, Todd Nelson, the Police Department now has ten reserve officers who will assist in the event of a local disaster. Currently, the Police, Fire Department and other emergency services are all coordinated to work together if the need should arise.

Although four emergency sirens are located around La Crescent, their effectiveness is limited to who can hear them, so the National Emergency Broadcast System on the TV and radio are the primary sources of alert and information for emergencies in the area. Meanwhile, the Reservists ride along with the Police, help with security and direct traffic at local events.

Information from interviews with Don Anderson & La Crescent Police Chief, Todd Nelson & from the 1966 *Civil Defense Adult Education Course Student Manual*.

CHAPTER 3:
GONE, BUT NOT FORGOTTEN

HERE LIES HARRY POTTER

La Crescent's *Real* Harry Potter

Young visitors to the Prospect Hill Cemetery in La Crescent are sometimes startled to find a gravestone with the name "Harry Potter". A century before the Harry Potter books, La Crescent really did have a resident named Harry Potter. Who was this Harry Potter? What was he like? What did he do? When did he live?

La Crescent's Harry Potter was a son of one of La Crescent's early settlers, Whitman and Hannah (Payne) Potter, who settled here in 1864, the year Harry was born.

According to his obituary, Harry's father, Whitman "...had taken one of the most prominent parts of all the affairs of the village..." and "...was also well known in La Crosse and possessed a considerable amount of property in [*La Crosse and La Crescent*]." Whitman Potter was born in Willington, Conn., July 13, 1834 and died June 4, 1911.

Harry's mother, Hannah, was born in Massachusetts on February 26, 1839 and was the daughter of Mr. And Mrs. John Payne, natives of England. She died September 6, 1917.

Harry had three known sisters, one of whose first name was not given, but when she married, she was known as Mrs. George Martin of Boston, Mass. The other two were: Mrs. C.W. (Cora) Turnbull of Albert Lee, Minn.; and Mrs. C.E. (Myrtle) Landers of Melrose, Wis. The first sister had died a year or two before Harry.

Harry "...had farmed in western Minnesota and at the time of death was engaged in farming in La Crescent..." according to his obituary. He died at the home of his mother, May 22, 1913 at the age

Harry Potter's gravestone in La Crescent's Prospect Hill Cemetery. [LA CRESCENT AREA HISTORICAL SOCIETY ARCHIVES – PHOTO BY DONNA HUEGEL]

of 49 "from affection of the brain illness, the illness having been brief in duration." He never married.

His parents moved here for unknown reasons during the Civil War. From the obituaries, we could guess that his family was fairly well to do, and Harry may have spoken with a bit of a British accent since his mother's family was from England. He probably had spats with his sisters growing up, as children do and they probably had fun times, too. Harry probably worked hard as an adult, as a farmer. We can only guess at what his interests and dreams were.

Although they were not listed in the obituaries as close relatives, there were other Potters also living in La Crescent in its early days. William Potter had a brick factory during the beginnings of La Crescent and built his brick house, which later became the Gittens' house in La Crescent near Bauer's Market. William Potter also built brick buildings and brick streets in La Crosse.

George Potter was also an early resident of La Crescent and was pictured as one of the original "Old Settlers" of the town that had regular reunion picnics for many years. The Prospect Hill Cemetery began from land given to the city by an early Potter family living in La Crescent.

Currently, no Potters are listed in La Crescent in the phone book, although there are several Potters listed in La Crosse and one in Hokah. None are known to have magical powers.

Information from La Crescent obituaries in the archives of the La Crescent Area Historical Society.

DEARLY BELOVED

Snippets from the Past in Area Cemeteries

A lot can be learned from area cemeteries, like the names of people who lived in the area, when they lived, perhaps information about their relationship to relatives, sometimes a hint of how they died and occasionally, some personal information about the deceased, like their main interest during their lives.

The oldest cemetery in La Crescent is Prospect Hill with a lovely hill view of the town and the Mississippi River. It was originally the Potter Addition (from farm land of W.B. Potter, an early settler). It dates back to 1853 with a three-month old baby named James Mercer being the first buried there.

According to Peg Senn Wansley, who was formerly sexton of that cemetery, there were 1,019 graves by the year 1997. Some of those buried there were Civil War Veterans, and a few early graves are unmarked with the people buried there being unknown. Why some people have no markers is an unanswered question. Were the relatives too poor to afford one? Were the ones in unmarked graves found dead with no identification? Did the people living at that time think they would always remember where their family members or friends were buried and forget to pass the information down to following generations? Did they mark the graves with wooden markers that didn't stand up through the ravages of time? One can only wonder.

Inscriptions on the headstones, though they may not say a lot, are revealing. Among the inscriptions on the older tombstones are: "Arthur N. Atstey M.D. Born in Australia Dec. 18, 1839 Died Dec. 12 1884."; "Georg W. Son of D.W. & S.L. Johnson Drowned July 1, 1889 Aged 18 Yrs. 3 M's"; "Henry F. Marwell killed by cars [*Note: we assume railroad cars or street cars since the automobile was still in very early experimental stages then*] May 24, 1887 Aged 21 Yrs. 5 M's 1 Day" and "Robert J. Mumma Injured in R.R. disaster at Eagle Point,

Grave markers in the oldest part of Pine Creek Catholic Cemetery, west of La Crescent on County Highway 6. [LA CRESCENT AREA HISTORICAL SOCIETY ARCHIVES – PHOTO BY DONNA HUEGEL]

Iowa on C.N. & St. P. RY Sept. 19, 1887 Died Dec. 5, 1887 Aged 26 Yrs. 19 D's. Erected by his wife Emma Mumma".

Unfortunately although many of the old headstones are intricately carved with beautiful artwork and loving sentiments, they are made of a stone that has not stood up to the test of time. So the inscriptions on many are so worn away by the elements as to be unreadable. Many of the oldest are also overgrown with moss, covering names and other information.

The old Pine Creek Catholic Cemetery is graced with three tall, beautifully crafted metal cross markers inscribed in German in the section that is the final resting place of German immigrants. Another, area of tall stone monuments features inscriptions that noted many of the people had been born in this or that county in Ireland. Although there seems to be plenty of space left for burials, most of the cemetery is off limits, since whenever digging began for graves in that section human remains were discovered.

The Toledo Cemetery is another old one in the area, across from the Pine Creek Golf Course, also dating back to the 1850s. Theyson was the name on the earliest marker there. Emil Theyson of the 3rd Wisconsin Infantry was a veteran of the Spanish American War.

The most common sentiment on grave markers there is: "Gone But Not Forgotten." Are they?

Information from Peg Wansley and garnered by walking through area cemeteries.

THE MYSTERY OF PINE CREEK CATHOLIC CEMETERY

Unknown Graves

The old Pine Creek Catholic Cemetery tells a tale of tragic sadness in La Crescent's history. Here is where family members buried many people in a hurry, as local lore goes, some in the middle of the night and many without markers, in an effort to stem a terrible deadly epidemic. Although there doesn't appear to be a lot of people buried there, an entire large section of the cemetery can not be used because grave digging turns up human remains. Thus, that area of the cemetery was declared off limits in 1984 or 1985.

In times of epidemics, funerals or public gatherings of any kind, including church services, were banned for fear of spreading the deadly diseases. So, as soon as soon as people died during area epidemics of diphtheria, cholera and other diseases from the 1850s into the 1880s, or possibly the Spanish Influenza of 1918, they were buried without funerals.

According to area historian, Anita Palmquist, before 1900 many burials were not recorded and especially on small farm plots, there were not even headstones to mark the spots of the dearly departed. Mostly, just the relatives knew where the graves were. Sometimes there were references to someone's death in old newspapers, but there weren't necessarily records or tombstones marking the date of death or place of the burial.

To compound the problem, there are no records of burials at this cemetery before 1878, although the cemetery is one of the oldest in the area. It dates back to 1853 when Martin Cody donated the land for a church and cemetery, according to the 1882 *History of Houston County*. (An old log school was used in the area for temporary Catholic services, but the first and subsequent Catholic churches were actually built in La Crescent.) It states: "A Mr. Morris who froze to death in the winter of 1856 was the first person to be buried in that cemetery." The oldest tombstone is for John Flanagan, born in County Galway, Ireland, who died August 1, 1857.

Quite likely, the early church records for the Pine Creek Catholic Cemetery were lost along with other church records when a fire destroyed the convent and attached Catholic school in La Crescent in 1906. A history of The Church of the Crucifixion stated that the fire broke out one night during evening mission devotions. A man burst into the church shouting, "The school is on fire! The school is on fire!" ending the sermon as volunteers rushed out to fight the fire. Nothing was saved.

A new monument placed in the Pine Creek Catholic Cemetery in 2003 is a memorial to the unknown people buried in unmarked graves in what appears to be an unused part of the cemetery in the background. The deceased are thought to be victims of a devastating diphtheria epidemic of 1874. [LA CRESCENT AREA HISTORICAL SOCIETY ARCHIVES – PHOTO BY DONNA HUEGEL]

So, tragically, besides not knowing when or why this section of the cemetery was mysteriously filled, even the names of the early settlers -- probably mostly children, who were buried there have been lost.

[*Note: After further investigation, the author turned up more information. Since then, in November of 2003, the La Crescent Area Historical Society has erected a monument to the unknown people buried in this cemetery.*]

It reads:

"This monument marks a tragic time in La Crescent's history and is a memorial to the unknown people buried in this area of the cemetery in unmarked graves. It is thought that the undetermined number of people buried here died during a diphtheria epidemic of 1874. To stem the epidemic people were buried without funerals as soon as they died, even in the middle of the night. The majority of the victims were likely children.

"Church records of this cemetery before 1878 were lost in a fire in 1906. So the names of these people have been lost as well as information about them. May their anonymous souls rest in peace.

"Placed by the La Crescent Area Historical Society and the Church of the Crucifixion 2003."

Finally, after 130 years, the victims of that tragic time have a marker and are remembered.

Information from Anita Palmquist, Peg Wansley, *History of the Church of the Crucifixion* & the 1882 *History of Houston County*.

CHAPTER 4:
UP THE RIVER WITHOUT (AND WITH) A PADDLE

LA CRESCENT'S "WILD KATE"
Ferries of La Crescent and La Crosse

La Crescent's "Wild Kate" wasn't a person, but rather a ferry between La Crescent and La Crosse in the early years of La Crescent before there were railroad or wagon bridges. It ran from La Crosse, Wisconsin across the Mississippi River to what is now Shore Acres in La Crescent.

The old road that runs from Shore Acres to what is now the foot of Main Street (in those days, called Mississippi Street) was the road to the city from Minnesota's shore. It had to be built up by hand with horses, men and countless shovels of dirt in the swampy area through Shore Acres to the town. This became the route used by immigrants, settlers and stagecoach travelers to La Crescent from La Crosse.

The *Wild Kate* was a public ferry, which started in 1854 and was run, literally, by horsepower. William McSpadden, who was a La Crosse hotel keeper, operated it. The ferry was so-dubbed because of its erratic and unpredictable schedule.

That same year, another public ferry, the *Honeoye*, ran from the foot of State Street in La Crosse across the Mississippi River to a point below the present (1876) railroad swing bridge on Shore Acres. This ferry came into the control of Thomas McRoberts, western representative of the Kentucky Company that built 12 houses in La Crescent, and gave the city its present name.

McRoberts won a charter from the Minnesota legislature giving

The ferry "Warsaw" used in the early days of transporting people across the Mississippi River between La Crescent, Minnesota and La Crosse, Wisconsin. Ferries were used from the 1850s until c.1890s. [LA CRESCENT AREA HISTORICAL SOCIETY ARCHIVES]

him exclusive privilege of operating ferries in Minnesota from the southern boundary of Winona County to the mouth of the Root River. Meanwhile, the Wisconsin legislature also granted him a limited charter to operate from La Crosse to the Minnesota shore.

Once having a monopoly on ferry service in the area, the Kentucky Company charged exorbitant prices to cross. ($1.10 to $1.50 per team of horses or oxen) Wages at that time were frequently $1.00 per day for labor. Public outrage led to a new ferry service running between La Crosse and Target Lake in La Crescent with a boat called the *General Pope*.

McRoberts brought a lawsuit against the operators in Minnesota courts and the *General Pope* was forced to suspend operation. Then McRoberts finally lowered his rates to 20 cents for a six-ox team and began to carry passengers for free. The ferry service continued until 1891 when a wagon bridge was built across the Mississippi River from Mt. Vernon Street in La Crosse to Minnesota. (That was the bridge preceding the Cass Street Bridge in La Crosse.)

[*Note: The ferry road is presently being studied by the Historic Preservation Commission of La Crescent for designation as an historic site, with hopes of it becoming a bicycle and pedestrian trail.*]

Information from research by Hugh McDowell; the 1919 History of Houston County

CHUG-CHUG, CHOO-CHOO, OFF WE GO
Mississippi River Railroad Swing Bridge

Look south from the Mississippi River Bridge

on I-90, or as you're headed south to La Crescent on Highway 61. Or look upriver as you cross the West Channel Bridge. You'll see it – the railroad swing bridge at the Shore Acres part of La Crescent. It has been part of the landscape for so long that we take it for granted.

Built in 1875 – 1876, the swing bridge is one of the oldest structures in the La Crescent area. It was a great improvement in transportation to this part of Minnesota. Previous to this bridge, boats or ferries across the river were the only transportation from the eastern United States to this area when the river wasn't frozen solid enough to travel across.

The railroad eventually crossed Wisconsin to La Crosse in 1858, where it met the great obstacle of the Mississippi. By 1868 the Root River Valley and Southern Minnesota Railroad had been built as far west as Lanesboro on the Minnesota side of the river. The problem was connecting the two.

A railroad ferry business was begun in 1865 from La Crosse to La Crescent, across the Mississippi River at a point known as "Grand Crossing". In the winter a route was established with tracks laid on islands as much as possible and then across the ice.

Until 1870, freight transferred from the Milwaukee and St. Paul Railroad to the Southern Minnesota Railroad was loaded and unloaded by hand. Then barges were constructed so whole railroad cars could be loaded onto the barges and ferried. At first, only one barge crossed, carrying four railroad cars at a time. Soon two barges were sent at a time with eight cars in each trip.

An 1875 news item reported that at least 16 round trips were made with eight cars each for a total of 156 cars transported across the busy river in one day. Transfer charges in 1873 were: $6.00 for loaded cars; $4.00 for empties, and 25 cents for passenger fares at a time when they ferried approximately 100 passengers a day plus freight.

In 1876 the Mc Donald Brothers of La Crosse built even bigger barges capable of carrying six cars each. But the process was still slow and tedious.

A paddle boat goes through the Mississippi River railroad swing bridge at La Crescent c. late 1800s. The bridge has been in constant use since it was built c.1876. It is one of the last of its kind left on the Mississippi River. [LA CRESCENT AREA HISTORICAL SOCIETY ARCHIVES – COURTESY OF DONALD ANDERSON]

Although the "new" railroad bridge was finished in November of 1876, ferries were still used until 1879. In 1890 the "Grand Crossing" site was abandoned.

The swing bridge at milepost 700 on the Mississippi River was made of wood initially and was powered by steam. The center pier of the bridge had a roller assembly. Each roller had a rod connected to a center pin, which kept rollers in the same track. The boiler was in the control house of the swing span. Coal had to be hauled out to the control house by wheelbarrow from a coal shed on the Minnesota side of the river.

By 1902 the bridge was reinforced with iron. It took two extra men on each shift. The two men had to remove rails from both ends

ONALASKA

LA CROSSE, TREMPEALEAU & PRESCOTT R.R.

FRENCH ISLAND

BLACK RIVER

MILWAUKEE & ST. PAUL R.R.

RIVER

MISSISSIPPI RIVER

NORTH LA CROSSE

LA CROSSE

N

WINTER ROUTE (TRACKS ON ICE)

LA CROSSE

GRAND CROSSING

SUMMER ROUTE (FERRY)

TARGET LAKE

MISSISSIPPI RIVER

SOUTHERN MINNESOTA R.R.

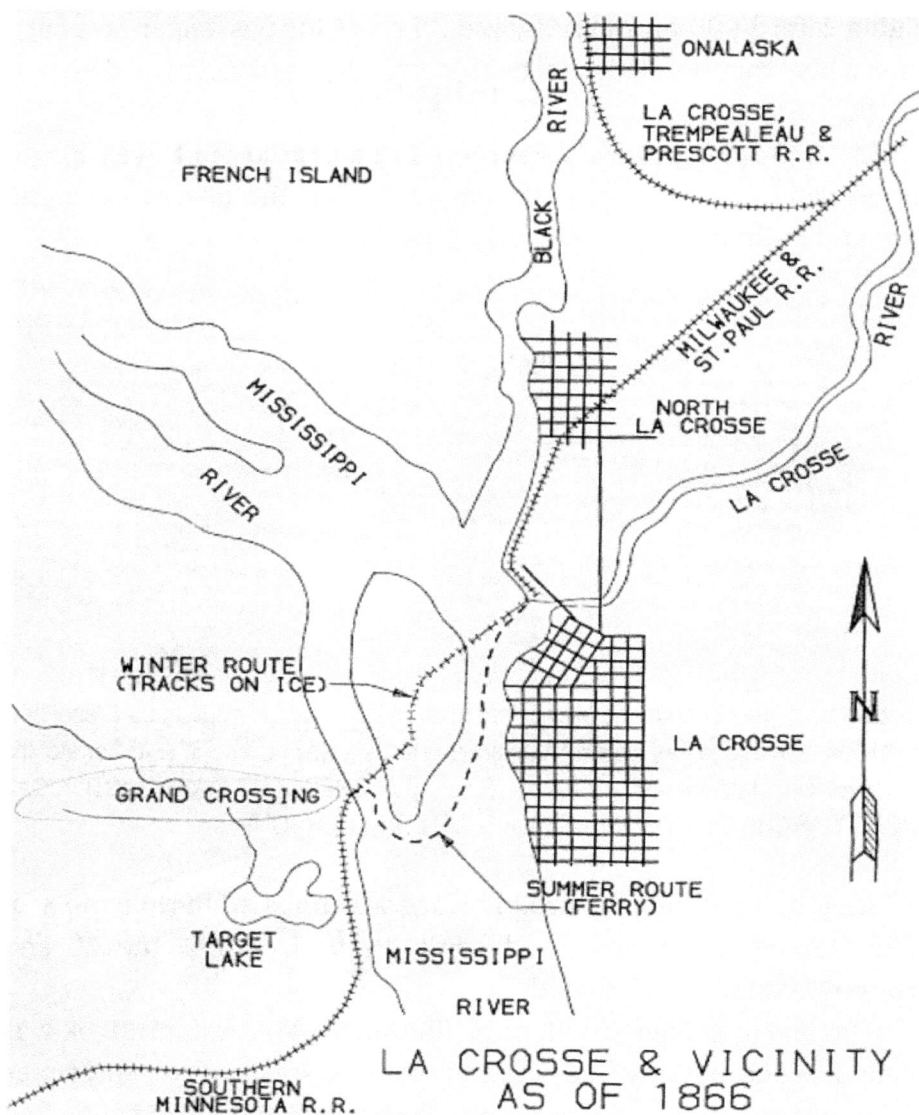

LA CROSSE & VICINITY AS OF 1866

A map of "Grand Crossing" on the Mississippi River, between La Crescent, Minnesota and La Crosse, Wisconsin. This is where railroad cars were ferried across the river before the railroad swing bridge was built c.1876 to connect the railroad of the eastern United States with the new western states. The map also indicates a winter ice route across the river for the railroad. [LA CRESCENT AREA HISTORICAL SOCIETY ARCHIVES – COURTESY OF INGRID FOWLER] of the swing bridge by hand and also crank up what they called "smash boards". When these were in the "up" position they indicated to train engineers to stop because the bridge was open for river traffic.

A tower extended up from each end of the swing span. They each displayed a kerosene lantern for riverboat pilots. In each lantern were two panels for red glass and two panels of green to indicate the position of the bridge – red for closed; green for open. The bridge tender could also signal boats with a steam whistle. Five short blasts meant a closed bridge; one prolonged blast followed by one short signaled the bridge was open to river traffic.

An outdoor toilet below the control house on a protection fence crib, water tank, smoke stack and water pipe to the control house were removed in the winter of 1952-1953 when the bridge was electrified and a new control house was added. In case of electrical failure, the bridge could be opened by hand in emergency. This took about four men to do.

The 1876 swing bridge is very unique in this day and age...not only because it's *still* in use after more than 125 years, but also because it's one of the last of its kind on the entire Mississippi River. It is considered an historical landmark by the state of Minnesota, but still requires local designation to be formally considered an historical site.

Information from written work by the late Don Fowler, donated materials from Donald Anderson (a former swing bridge tender) and undated newspaper article.

CHAPTER 5:
HOW YOU SAY, "AMERIKA"

BOOM TO BUST
Brownsville, Minnesota – An Immigrant Port

Brownsville, Minnesota today is only a shadow of its former self. In its early days pioneers were eager to settle west of the Mississippi River, looking for land to call their own or to start their own businesses. German, Irish and Norwegian immigrants, as well as settlers from the eastern U.S., traveling up the Mississippi River disembarked at Brownsville because of its natural port.

According to the 1919 *History of Houston County*, Brownsville was settled in 1848 by Job Brown and two wanderers whom he encountered living on an island in the river. The site of the village was at the foot of Wild Cat Bluff, nearly 500 feet high, which was the high point on the river for miles, and was a prominent landmark for the early river pilots and steamboat captains. The landing there became the point of debarkation for a large number of the pioneer settlers, especially those going to Caledonia and vicinity.

In the winter of 1848 Job brought in his brother, Charles Brown, and his brother-in-law, James Hiner, as well as some helpers. In 1850 came David Brown, not a relative of the other Browns. A little later came William Morrison (better known as "Wild Cat Jack") and William Blair. These men all settled in the village and there the history of the township has since centered.

The first building was made of logs, moved down from an island opposite the mouth of the Root River. It measured 14 by 12 feet and had a "shaker" roof. It was described as being "about 300 yards above the stone warehouse."

Charles Brown erected the first frame building in 1850 and it was afterwards used as a schoolhouse. Mr. Brown also built the first public building, which had multiple uses. It was called the town hall, but it was also used as both a Methodist and Episcopal Church, as well as a schoolhouse.

Smith's Hotel in Brownsville possibly before the town's decline in the 1880s. Many of the early businesses in the once thriving immigrant port no longer exist. [LA CRESCENT AREA HISTORICAL SOCIETY ARCHIVES]

Imagine the scene as the 1919 *History of Houston County* stated: "In 1855 the levee was crowded with goods and during the quarter ending June 30 the land sales amounted to $74,292. The census then gave the county a population of 2,616. There was a theater in successful operation in the village and lots were selling from $100 to $800 each. At the beginning of this year the population of the village was 50 inhabitants and there were 20 offices and stores, but by the end of the year there were 228 inhabitants and 45 new buildings had been erected. In the fall a Sunday school was started in the store of Gates & Wykoff.

"On July 1, 1856, several stage lines were started, carrying mail; one from Brownsville to Chatfield, via Hokah, Houston and Rushford; another from Brownsville to Caledonia, via Elliota and a third from Brownsville to Traverse de Sioux..."

The history continued, "In 1870 there were nearly fifty stores in active operation, but in 1882 there were not more than half as many places of business, including saloons and shops. The following is a fairly comprehensive list: A.L. Darling, general merchandise and hardware; John H. Rippe, general merchandise; John Cluss, hardware; Frank P. Moore, drugs; Miss T. M. Dorival, millinery and fancy goods; Aug. Knautz, boots, shoes and harness; Thomas Curry, grocery and shoemaker; Leonard Schwartz, meat market; Edmund Kelly, groceries and liquors; William Tohman, groceries and liquors; William Powers, general merchandise; John C. Beck, wagon and carriage maker; William Idecker, blacksmith; James Collern; Gustavus Graf, blacksmith; Adolf Rier, carpenter and cabinetmaker; F. Brehme, barber, confectionery and toys; Matt Roster, Fred Gluck, Peter Thimmersch, Florian Hauber and George Hoffman, saloon keepers; Michael Feeney, groceries and meat market; John Rippe, agent for the Diamond Jo, salt, cement and lime. There were three principal hotels: the Gluck House, conducted by Fred Gluck; the Roster House, by Matt Roster and the Minnesota House, besides several smaller public houses.

"In the winter of the same year a St. Louis firm made arrangements for cutting 10,000 tons of ice above the village. At this time the town had two physicians, Dr. J. M. Riley and Dr. W. W. Bell."

Several manufacturing industries were also established in the village and its vicinity. Some were: the Brownsville Knoblack Brewery (which in 1856 could not keep up with demand), Wild Cat Flouring Mill, City Flour Mill, Brownsville Bluff Brewery, Clark's sawmill, the Job and Charles Brown grist mill and several attempts at lead mining.

Driving through the sleepy community of Brownville now, it's hard to imagine it as the busy center of commerce it once was, like so many other small towns were nearly 150 years ago.

Information from the 1919 *History of Houston County*.

NO ONE KNOWS IF HE GOT A WIFE
Brownsville – Ice Route Across the Mississippi River

In the winter of the year when the Mississippi River is usually frozen, it served other purposes back in the 1800s. No doubt, then, as now there were ice fishermen. Some of the ice was "harvested" into blocks to store in icehouses for use in the summer. And the frozen river made winter travel across it as easy as walking or taking horses.

But someone had to find the safest places to cross and mark the route. In the late 1800s, one of those men was George Holzheimer, who was known as the "Ice King" for laying out ice roads between La Crosse, Wisconsin and Brownsville, Minnesota. He was known to walk the streets "without the least precaution against the cold" during "the most bitter winter weather". In undated news clipping, a notice was given about his retirement party. The article in the *Hokah Chief* newspaper read:

QUEER SORT OF ANNIVERSARY

The 25th of this month, George Holzheimer informed us, it will be twenty-five years since he first commenced to stake out roads on the Mississippi from Brownsville to La Crosse and from thence to the Minnesota side and on that day he will enjoy a holiday.

He will invite friends from Brownsville, La Crosse and Hokah to help him enjoy a pleasant time in the way of serving dinner, drinking beer and having a general good time and that after that day, on account of old age, he will resign his position and settle down to a more comfortable life. He is a nice pleasant old gentleman and has many warm friends in Houston County. To the person following him he will give all the information regarding the color of ice as to safety, etc. free of charge.

NOTICE

To all whom it may concern: Since I have laid out roads on the ice for the last twenty years, I will celebrate my ice wedding Tuesday, January 15th next, at the Town Hall in Hokah, Minnesota. To make the affair more interesting I offer $50 cash to any lady in Wisconsin, Minnesota or Iowa that can beat me dancing a waltz, but if she fails she is to become my wife. – Geo. Holzheimer

There was no follow up story to be found as to whether he got any takers on this offer...or a wife. But he sure knew how to make a party interesting!

Information from undated article in the *Hokah Chief.*

CHAPTER 6:
SENT UP THE RIVER
GONE TO THE GREAT
HUNTING GROUND IN THE SKY
Memories of a Dresbach, Minnesota Pioneer

Joseph Robillard came to Dresbach, Minnesota with his family at the age of five in 1851 and grew up there on the banks of the Mississippi River. At the age of 75, he recounted some of his pioneer memories to the *La Crosse Tribune and Leader-Press* in 1920. The following are stories and excerpts from that news article.

Robillard's grandfather came to the area first and persuaded Joseph's parents, Rachel and Lambert Robillard to relocate here from Freeport, IL. Joseph's brother, Wilfred, was the first white child born in Winona County in 1853. They lived in a little log cabin they built, 16 feet long and 12 feet wide. The structure had no floor but the hard clay ground. The next thing Joseph's father did was to clear the land of brush and trees and make a small garden plot. There were several other settlers in the vicinity then, but they were quite a distance apart from one another.

Robillard told of his first encounter with an Indian his first winter there:

"I will never forget how frightened I was. We were visiting at a neighboring settler's cabin and my grandfather, his friend and myself decided to go back into the woods and visit the wood-choppers who lived in the shanties and who cut wood for their living.

As we entered one cabin I saw an Indian, stripped to the waist, and smeared with red and yellow paint. He was squeezing a piece of lead between his teeth and trying to make it small enough to fit in his gun.

The first white settlers of the area encountered some remaining Native Americans and witnessed some of their rituals. [OURSELVES AND OUR CITY – SCHOOL TEXT BOOK OF 1928]

"That was enough for me; I gave one whoop and ran into the woods as fast as I could. I thought that the Indian was coming after me to get my scalp. I was only five years old then and I thought that all Indians were warriors. I don't know how far I had run but when I stopped, all out of breath, I heard someone calling me. I answered and then I saw my grandfather and his friend coming in my direction, laughing heartily. They told me that the Indian I saw was nothing but a peace-loving Winnebago and that he would not harm little boys for anything in the world."

About life along the river, Robillard said, there were "all kinds of fish in the river that seemed glad to swallow a bent wire at the end of a hickory pole." There were also "lots of kids to go swimmin' with at any time of day and the old lumber rafts to dive off."

"Our cabin was only a little way from the river, and often on a summer night, my friends and I would lie on the banks of the river and watch the old packet steamers pass up and down the river. We could see the pilot sitting in his luxuriously furnished cabin guiding the boat wherever he wanted it to go, and hear the old Negroes singing 'Weep No More My Lady' and 'Way Down Upon the 'Suwanne Ribber'."

Robillard continued:

"The beast of burden when we moved to Dresbach was the oxen, and in 1853 my grandfather Maynard journeyed to Canada by an old cart and a yoke of oxen. He met several Frenchmen while there and told them of French Island and of the beautiful country in southern Minnesota. In the spring of [18]'55 those Frenchmen moved to the island and settled there. Among them were the Jolivettes, LaBelles, Goyettes, Richmonds and LaNores.

"The Goyettes and Jolivettes had boys about my size and we often played together. I was visiting at their house on the island one time and while there I saw an Indian funeral. It is the only real Indian funeral I ever saw. The Indians placed the body in the grave and rode around the grave chanting a peculiar hymn. They put all of the dead man's weapons in the grave and covered him up after marching around the grave for about a half an hour.

"My father was one of the first men to own a horse. One day the animal was stolen, and my father almost worried himself sick over the loss. An uncle of mine ran a wagon and blacksmith shop at Dubuque, (Iowa) and my father wrote to him to keep a watch for the animal. About a week later my uncle wrote to him that the horse had been brought to his shop to be shod and that he knew where the man that had the horse lived. My father set out on foot immediately for Dubuque and when he reached there he identified the animal as his and rode him home.

"A few years later my father and grandfather sold their land to George B. Dresbach, and then they built a hotel. The hotel was in use for many years, it being a favorite resting place among the travelers and the men who drove the sleighs up river carrying food and mail during the winter."

Dresbach, Minnesota has seen many changes since those earliest days of White settlement. There's just no better way to learn of its beginning days than to hear it from the people who lived it.

Information from 1920 *La Crosse Tribune and Leader-Press*.

WING DAM BATTLE
Dresbach and Dakota, Minnesota Take on the Government

May 30, 1912 the citizens of Dakota and Dresbach petitioned Congress, demanding the government go over the head of the War Department to investigate a six-year-old quarrel. The problem? Wing dams on the Mississippi River.

The two villages asserted that since the War Department put the wing dams in place, they had been cut off from the river. They maintained that the wing dams had created "an immense sandbar" in front of Dakota, causing problems of water stagnation and deprived them of "every steamboat landing which could be approached by wagon." They also said the wing dams caused the loss of many acres of meadowlands on the Wisconsin shore.

People on the Wisconsin side of the river at this time, were also asking the state of Wisconsin to sue the federal government for damages by destruction of valuable land when the river channel was shifted.

The citizens of Dresbach and Dakota wanted the channel put back the way it formerly was in 1878. They argued, "The natural channel of the river is along the rocky Minnesota side, where the bluffs come down to the water's edge, and not along the Wisconsin side, where for miles inland the land is low and marshy." "The result of the wing dam," they said, was "the shore of the river has been built up further and further from the old Minnesota shore line and the landings have become useless."

Captain W.A. Thompson, a local representative of the War Department, responded that "The course of the river has only been deflected enough to straighten out unnecessary kinks in the channel, which caused boats to zig-zag needlessly from side to side." Although he admitted that some damage had been done to Dresbach and Dakota from the wing dams, he concluded, "a few dredgings will give the protesting two villages better steamboat landings than they have had in thirty-five years... "To tear out the work and allow the river to go back to the old place would mean destruction of $200,000 worth of work and the expenditure of nearly as much destroying it."

A car travels south of Dresbach, Minnesota along the Mississippi River in 1924. This road later became Highway 61 (part of I-90 is now in this stretch of the road). Dresbach and Dakota, Minnesota dwindled as towns after their river ports silted in from the wing dams built to improve navigation on the Mississippi. [LA CRESCENT AREA HISTORICAL SOCIETY ARCHIVES]

At the request of Dakota and Dresbach, Congressman Sydney Anderson of that district looked into the matter and was satisfied that the work was done correctly. He stated that the work "transformed a crooked and shallow channel (less than three feet in places) into one satisfying the demands of the approved six-foot project."

The citizens of Dakota and Dresbach were left disappointed as the government finally concluded that the work completed was actually the most successful project of its kind on the river, and the wing dams were left in place.

Information from undated news clipping (probably 1912) of unknown local newspaper.

NOT ENOUGH COAXING
Dresbach & Dakota, Minnesota in 1928

Dresbach and Dakota started out as towns depending on river travel for their growth. Their natural ports filled in with sand following the construction of wing dams on the river in 1878 and subsequent improvements for river commerce. So the two towns struggled.

By 1928 they tried to pool their resources in hopes of helping the towns to grow. They formed the "D. and D. Unity Club". On October 17th of that year, they held a chicken dinner and dance at the Dresbach Centennial Hall, with proceeds going toward the purchase of the community park and playground land. On December 28, 1928 the *D. and D. Unity News* debuted. The aim of the publication, it said, was "to further community spirit between the villages of Dakota and Dresbach and the surrounding country." It continued, "It is hoped thereby to stimulate and arouse the efforts of the citizens in the projects planned for the welfare and development of these communities. Let's all put our shoulder to the wheel and put Dakota and Dresbach on the map as they never were before."

Little blurbs were scattered throughout the publication, "Patronize the advertisers in the *D. & D. Unity News*." The local businesses that advertised in that first issue were from Dresbach: Jonah Husmann Cash Store – "Radiola Sales and Service, fancy groceries a specialty, pasteurized milk and meats"; D.H. Baker & Son, "dealers in livestock, flour, sugar and grain"; A.E. Webster "for reliable auto and fire insurance"; and George Moore, who was selling *"McConnon's* Cough Mixture and Rheumual".

The advertisers from Dakota were: Dakota Garage, proclaiming: "Will have on display January 1st the New *Chevrolet Six*"; Donehower

Store offered "a nice calendar" for its customers as well as special holiday values in candies, nuts, a variety of fruits and vegetables, Baltimore oysters, dressed poultry, etc.; the Mississippi Valley Co-op Creamery Assn.; the E.F. Baker *Standard Oil Co.* Station which reminded people to drain and flush their crankcases and transmissions and refill them with the correct grade of *Polarine* and

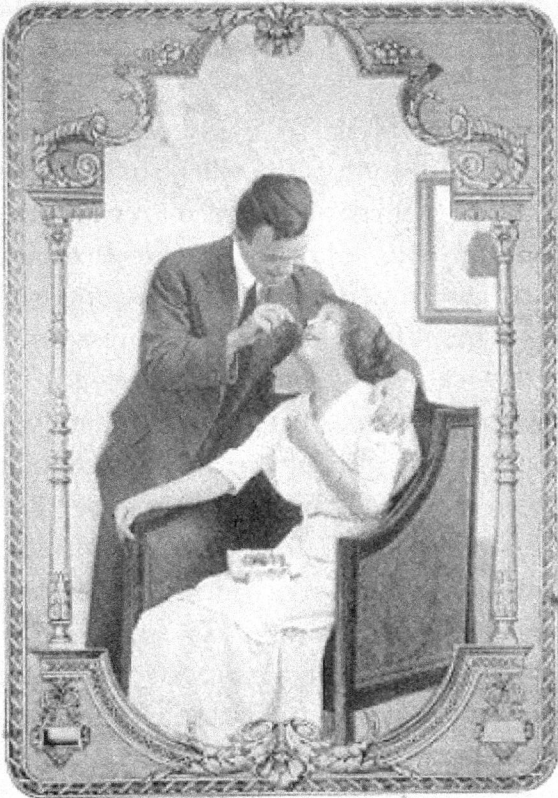

You need some coaxing

in DAKOTA, MINN.

A postcard from Dakota, Minnesota with a postmark of 1920. Dakota and Dresbach, Minnesota struggled to stay alive in the 1920s and attempted to renew interest in the two neighboring towns. [LA CRESCENT AREA HISTORICAL SOCIETY ARCHIVES – COURTESY OF DONNA HUEGEL]

Iso-vis, and "protect your radiator with alcohol". It also mentioned "free air and rest room". The Dakota State Bank boasted total resources over $600,000 and offered 4% interest paid on time deposits; E.L. Brown General Merchandise simply said, "Come in and look over our Christmas stock." Ernest C. Waldow had a funeral and embalming service and Chris. Trocinski sold *McCormick, Deering and John Deer* Farm Implements, *Maytag* Washers and *DeLaval* Separators.

Among local news mentioned was: "A light tower for the guidance of aircraft has been erected south of the village of Dresbach at the brow of Ready hill..." In sports: "The second victorious basketball game of the season was played by the Dresbach ("Maroons") team Saturday evening at Centennial hall. The opposing team was the Vocational school quint from La Crosse...Admission 10 and 25 cents." Skating on the ice "was pronounced perfect", the Dresbach School was preparing a Christmas program and there was to be a Christmas cantata sung by the girls of the Sunday school at the Dresbach Methodist church on Sunday evening, December 23rd. Clarence Gile had just returned from Pierre, S.D. "where he drove a new automobile which he delivered to Harry Horner" and other small town events such as socializing and visiting.

The issue also covered a "simple but very impressive" wedding at the home of Mr. And Mrs. Wm. Harrington, Saturday afternoon, Dec. 8th of their daughter, Lucile to Maurice Johnson of Hastings, Minn. It said, "Before the ceremony 'At Dawning' was sung by Mrs. Marion Holtze Hilton of La Crosse, who also played Lohengren's wedding march which heralded the approach of the bridal party as they descended the stairs to an improvised altar in the living room where the bride was given away by her father. The bride wore a gown of turquoise blue transparent velvet and her attendant was in pale green satin crepe, both carrying arm bouquets of pink roses and sweet peas...The decorations throughout all the rooms were beautiful and a pink and white effect was the color scheme.."

Dresbach and Dakota still haven't achieved their goal of growing into booming metropolises. Perhaps timing was part of the problem since all the Christmas ads in the D *& D Unity News* didn't appear until December 28th or later...or maybe there just wasn't enough coaxing.

Information from the *D & D Unity News*, Dec. 28, 1928.

CHAPTER 7:
AN 1800s TOURIST TOWN
WELCOME TO LAKE COMO
Hokah, Minnesota's Popular Resort

Where did the masses of people flock to on a hot summer day a hundred years ago? Lake Como at Hokah, Minnesota, of course! The prettiest little summer resort town around in the exciting new West of the late 1800s and early 1900s. The Mississippi River was far too busy then with river commerce, so the place in which to get away for relaxation and quiet was scenic Lake Como...at least until it was the "in" place to go and became very crowded.

Lake Como was made in the 1850s when Thompson Creek, running through Hokah and bordered by 26 springs, was dammed up for Edward Thompson's saw and flourmills. The lake filled the valley to the south of the main street (Hwy. 44) where the Hokah baseball field is now.

It became a popular summer resort in the 1890s when Pro Steven, a La Crosse, Wisconsin man, moved there and developed it. He had a little cottage on the peninsula extending into the lake from the south shore, near where the bridge is now. He built a pavilion and several rustic cottages on the peninsula, established a bathing beach and provided boats for passengers, a flat boat equipped with wide side wheels which turned by hand, rowboats, canoes and fishing tackle. Then he invited summer visitors.

Although roads to Hokah were poor and even impassable at times by horse and wagon, making the journey two hours from La Crosse, it was trains that brought tourists from La Crosse and even Chicago to the popular resort town. George Kindhammer, (now deceased) an elderly life-long Hokah resident had said hundreds of people would roam the streets of Hokah (currently a population of 614) on a Sunday afternoon enjoying the beauty of the area on their vacations and picnics around the turn of the 20ᵗʰ Century.

Lake Como taken from Mount Tom in Hokah, Minnesota probably from its early days before the original lake disappeared in a 1909 flood when a dam washed out after a heavy rain. The lake returned in 1922 when Thompson Creek was dammed up again, but by 1936 it had filled in from silt due to poor environmental practices of farming at the time. [LA CRESCENT AREA HISTORICAL SOCIETY ARCHIVES]

Lake Como disappeared on August 14, 1909 when the dam washed out in a big flood. Interest was rekindled in rebuilding the resort by several Hokah men after a new "automobile road" was built between La Crescent and Hokah around 1920, making the trip from La Crosse to Hokah only 20-25 minutes by car. The lake was rebuilt in 1922 as a resort with shore land plotted for cottages and also the creation of a new hotel, a dancing pavilion, boat livery and various concessions.

By 1936 nearby hills stripped of timber and damaged by farm animals had been eroded by water carrying sand and clay down from the hills, gradually filling the lake with sediment. The resort was abandoned. All that remains of it now is the Hokah swimming pool with its sandy bottom at the east end on the former Pendergast grounds from the days of Lake Como.

Thompson Creek still runs through the valley, however, and the Como Falls still exist from the east end of Lake Como, beyond the Hokah swimming pool. A city park was developed at the foot of Como Falls in the 1990s and it is accessible from the Fire Department parking lot.

Information from old newspaper clippings, photographs and George Kindhammer.

GETTING OFF THE TRACK

Hokah Train Wreck

The date was March 14, 1913. It was the middle of the night along the banks of the Root River about three miles west of Hokah. After an unusually heavy downpour, the sandy banks below the railroad tracks gave way. Without warning, train no. 8 plunged into a washout eight to ten feet deep and 600 feet long.

The newspaper account read in part:

> Wreck of Train No. 8
> Engine Sinks into Huge Hole and is Buried,
> Tender Smashing Through Cab and Piling on top
> FIREMEN KILLED – ENGINEER INJURED
> Wreck Caused by Quicksand's Giving Way Under Track.
> None of Passengers Hurt

> Eastbound passenger train No. 8, due here at 10:55 p.m. met with a shocking accident nearly three miles west of Hokah, Friday morning at 2:40 o'clock, in which Engineer Charles Whiting was seriously injured and Fireman Newton Nelson lost his life.

> News of the wreck was first received at the home of James Holliday, near the scene of the accident, and at about four o'clock when Conductor Murphy summoned Dr. Ready.

> The relief train went up from La Crosse at the earliest possible opportunity, and found the situation thus: A washout under the track about the length of a rail and a half, and eight to ten feet deep about a quarter mile east of the 'yellow banks'. Into this hole the engine plunged and sunk, the tender leaving its

tracks and jackknifing over it. The mail car had shot its length ahead of the engine and partly tipped over, and the baggage car stood alongside of the engine. The coaches were not derailed.

The train wreck of March 14, 1913 three miles west of Hokah. The train derailed at 2:40 A.M. when a heavy rain washed out part of the tracks. [LA CRESCENT AREA HISTORICAL SOCIETY ARCHIVES]

Fireman Newton Nelson was found at his post, stone dead, and Engineer Chas. Whiting was found pinned fast, with his leg broken in two places below the knee, He was badly scalded by escaping steam but managed to keep most of it out of his face by holding up a board which fortunately was in reach. None of the other train passengers were injured.

The train was over three hours late, owing to being derailed for two and a half hours a few miles west of Houston, in another washout. This caused some damage to the engine, and Engineer Whiting was running slowly in consequence. But for this, the train

STEALING THE MISSISSIPPI RIVER

would have been running at high speed to make up time, and a catastrophe would no doubt have ensued.

The article continued with gory descriptions of the dead fireman's body, clean up of the wreck and another unrelated fatal railroad accident east of Caledonia.

The passenger trains stopped running on the railroad line long ago, and even the railroad tracks are now gone. A remnant of the old railroad is seen with posts of a bridge popping out of the water at the southwest corner of Highways 16 and 26, south of La Crescent. A bit of the railroad bed is visible near the posts. Some of this route from Houston, Minnesota on west is now converted to the Root River Bicycle Trail. Oh, the tales the hills and river could tell us – if they could only talk!

Information from a 1913 unknown local newspaper clipping.

CHAPTER 8:
READIN', 'RITIN' & 'RITHMETIC

TEACHERS WILL BRING A BUCKET OF WATER AND A PILE OF WOOD...
Rules for Teachers in 1858

Schools have undergone big changes in the United States. Gone are most of the rural one-room schools accommodating all eight grades that were the norm in the U.S. from its early days until the 1960s. Gone are the days of corporal punishment and dunce hats. Rules in the classroom have definitely changed – not only for students, but for the teachers as well. The following is a list of rules for *teachers* in 1858:

1. Teachers each day will fill lamps, clean chimneys.
2. Each teacher will bring a bucket of water and a pile of wood for the day's session. The families of the children will be asked to help with this endeavor.
3. Make your pens carefully. You may whittle nibs to the individual taste of pupils.
4. Men teachers may take one evening each week for courting purposes, or two evenings a week if they go to church regularly.
5. After ten hours in school, the teachers may spend the remaining time reading the Bible or other

good books.

6. Women teachers who marry or engage in unseemly conduct will be dismissed.

7. Every teacher should lay aside, from each pay, a goodly sum of their earnings for their benefit during their declining years so that they will not become a burden on society.

8. Any teacher who smokes, uses liquor in any form, frequents pool or public halls, or gets shaved in a barber shop will give good reason to suspect his worth, intention, integrity and honesty.

9. Teachers who perform their labor faithfully and without fault for five years will be given an increase of 25 cents per week in their pay, providing the Board of Education approves.

La Crescent's first school at 542 3rd Street north was built in 1857. The first year from six to ten students attended with Miss Nancy Ambler as their teacher. The school year lasted only three months due to a contagious fever that hit the area, so the school suspended classes for a time. The school still exists, but is unrecognizable as it has been a private residence for many years and has been remodeled a number of times. [LA CRESCENT AREA HISTORICAL SOCIETY ARCHIVES]

The wage scale for teachers in the 1850s was $122 per year. It was paid in increments three times a year: $50 in September, $22 in December and $50 in April.

Yes, indeed! Things have changed quite a bit for the teachers, as well as the students in the last 150 years.

Information from a flyer from the Rushford Historical Society.

"IF TWO STAGECOACHES ARE HEADED WEST..."

Textbooks of the 1860s – '70s

Education, among many other things has seen great changes in the last 100-plus years. Schooling has gone from slates to computers; from eight grades in tiny one-room schools to bussed mega-schools with hundreds of students in a single grade.

Throughout those years in education, the message itself has also become substantially different. What was considered important to know, as well as a glimpse of life itself, more than 100 years ago are revealed in the following excerpts from school textbooks of the 1860s and 1870s.

From page 65 of *Clark's First Grammar* (1868) are a sample of sentences to diagram:

"Evil communications always corrupt good manners."

"Good examples generally secure correct habits."

From page 71 of the same book, still concentrating on learning proper sentence structure:

"The habit of intemperance produces much lasting misery."

"The use of tobacco degrades many good men."

"The benevolence of God secures our highest good."

"Our systems of education elevate the human character."

From an 1877 *Ray's New Intellectual Arithmetic* book of math story problems, we get a glimpse of life at the time:

Page 34: "A stage starts from a certain town and travels at the rate of eight miles per hour: at the same time, another starts from the same place and travels in the same direction, four miles per hour: how far will they be apart at the end of 12 hours?"

Page 64: "If a carpenter earns $8 in five days, how much will he earn in nine days?"

"If one barrel of flour serves eight persons 20 days, how long will it last 11 persons?"

Page 139: "James was hired for 30 days: for every day he worked he was to receive 30 cents, and for every day he was idle he was to pay 20 cents for his board; at the end of the time he received $5: how many days did he work?"

Reading material from an 1872 *Sander's Union Fifth Reader* geared to about an 8th grade level included articles and poems on the subjects of work, soldiers, education, God, virtues and vices,

La Crescent's second school built of stone, in 1868. It burned down and was replaced at the same site with the "Old Brick School". The site is the present home of a branch of the State Bank of La Crosse at 109 S. Walnut. None of the people in the photograph have been identified. [LA CRESCENT AREA HISTORICAL SOCIETY ARCHIVES – COURTESY OF DON TURNBULL]

discoveries, historical figures and events, travel and beauty. Among the authors were Shakespeare and Tennyson; and articles included some from *Harper's Maga*zine and the *Saturday Evening Post* as well as excerpts from the *Bible*.

Some titles were *"There's Work Enough to Do"*, *"Where There's a Will, There's a Way,"* *"Desolating Effects of Intemperance,"* *"Beatitudes"* and *"Profaneness."*

The first paragraph in the article on "Profaneness" by E. H. Chapin reads:

> "Profaneness is a low, groveling vice. He who indulges in it is no gentleman. I care not what his stamp may be in society – I care not what clothes he wears or what culture he boasts – despite all his refinement, the light and habitual taking of God's name in vain betrays a coarse nature and a brutal will."

What do you suppose content of our current school textbooks will tell future generations about our lives and times?

Information from: *Clark's First Grammar* (1868), *Ray's New Intellectual Arithmetic* (1877), and *Sander's Union Fifth Reader* (1872).

LA CRESCENT'S FEMALE SEMINARY

La Crescent's Schools – Likely and Unlikely

Kids have been going back to school for 145 years in La Crescent. Although La Crescent was founded in 1851, populating the town was slow, and the first public school wasn't built until 1857. Classes actually were held for one term in a small frame building for about eight students in 1856, but that was only for three months as "the fever and ague [*Note: a fever with chills*] came along and shook the school up so lively that it was, for the time, discontinued" according the 1882 *History of Houston County*.

La Crescent's first public school located on N. Third St. was like most, a one-room schoolhouse, (20x30 feet) but was built substantially of brick and was used until 1868, when a larger school was needed and built. This little school was then used as a carpenter shop by W.R. Anderson and was later converted into a private residence.

In 1857 the public school had to compete with The Carr Academy, built at that time and run by Elder Spencer Carr, a Baptist Minister. The history remarked about it: "A building was erected with a view of enlarging it if necessary. The higher branches were taught, and some pupils from abroad were secured, which, with others in town, made up the number of about eighteen. The school was not an overwhelming success..." It soon was converted into a drugstore, and Elder Carr went to Wisconsin and finally to Kansas, "...where he paid the debt of mortality."

The La Crescent Female Seminary opened in town in 1861. According to the same source, Mrs. Rice, her son, Edwin, and Mrs. Anderson were the teachers. "...They first occupied a building put up by Charles Waller, of Chicago, ... and there was an attendance of from twenty to thirty pupils, the old La Crescent Hotel [*Note: near where the Post Office is now*] being used as a boarding house. After the first year the whole establishment was removed to the Hotel, using the whole building and from thirty to forty boarders were secured with several day scholars from the village. At the end of two years they removed to Rochester, and after awhile the family went to California."

Meanwhile public education continued in 1868, with the town's second public school, a two-story limestone structure, built on South Walnut, where a branch of the State Bank of La Crosse now sits. The limestone for the building was taken from the Potter and Taylor Quarries on the North Ridge road. It was 26 x 42 feet and built for $2,800. The students attended ten months of the year. It served the community and its approximately 80 students. It burned down and was replaced at the same site with the "Old Brick School" in 1905.

La Crescent's third school ("the Old Brick School") in 1918. This school was built at 109 S. Walnut in 1904-1906 by B. Linston Construction of La Crosse for $3,300. The school was built amid controversy and torn down amid controversy in the 1990s. The branch bank of the State Bank of La Crosse that now occupies the spot was built with architecture reminiscent of the Old Brick School. [LA CRESCENT AREA HISTORICAL SOCIETY ARCHIVES]

According to an account in a 1958 Applefest booklet, "During the years 1905-06, while the stone building was being wrecked and a new school being built (with much bickering and a lawsuit prolonging the procedure) the children in the primary grades and those in the seventh and eighth grades attended classes in rooms in the Kentucky Company's double store building [*Note: at 309 Main St.*]. The children in the middle grades went to another temporary schoolhouse near the present parochial school." In 1997, the "Old Brick School" was torn down as it started, in the midst of controversy.

The present public elementary school was built as a one-story structure in 1950. The second story was added by 1955 and accommodated students through eighth grade.

Nuns had conducted Catholic school in La Crescent in the 1890s, but then for over fifty years all children attended the public school. The Church of the Crucifixion Parochial School was built as a one-story building in 1950, also adding its second story by 1955 because of the baby boom. In 1957 the congregation added the auditorium.

The La Crescent public high school opened in 1965; giving the town it's first high school. Before that, students who went to school beyond eighth grade attended one of the high schools in La Crosse. The school was enlarged in 2000-01 to better accommodate middle school students as well.

Finally, the La Crescent Montessori Public Academy opened in 2000. One more place in La Crescent for students to go back to school.

Information from the 1882 *History of Houston County*, 1958 Applefest booklet, newspaper clippings and current information from La Crescent City Hall.

WHAT I DID ON MY SUMMER VACATION – 1896

Bits of News in 1896

Area students writing what they did during summer vacation for a school report in 1896 might have included some of these events, according to newspapers in La Crosse at the time.

On June 6 of 1896 they might have watched women playing baseball. A clipping stated: "A female baseball club, that practices industriously near Front and State streets during the noon hour, is attracting much attention. Some of the girls, who work in Front Street candy and laundry firms, exhibit much skill in the manner in which they play the great national game."

Maybe they had a stay at a "Bicycle Hotel" that opened at 829 Green Bay Street on June 15 of that year. It provided refreshments and accommodations, as well as tools and a large air pump for the benefit of the bicyclists.

Perhaps the vacation started a little later as June 26 was graduation day from La Crosse High School with 19 girls and 8 boys graduating.

On June 27 La Crosse had a "Ladies Day" which the kids could have attended. Local women served as conductors on the electric streetcars and received a share of the collected fares. "The female conductors created a sensation around town," the article said, "and the streets were crowded with people out 'to see the show'. The streetcars were decorated with flags, bunting, and colored paper for the event which saw 5,757 passengers carried by the ladies, earning them a profit of about $100 for the day."

The children may have been pestered by the July 1 return of the mayflies. The newspaper commented: "During the evening the city is subjected to its annual visit by those soft, nasty, stinking insects known as mayflies. Like the sands of the oceans were their numbers and they made an excellent imitation of a snow storm around every exposed light, driving all humanity indoors in the process."

The Fourth of July was an event more to participate in than watch, as it was noted that it was "one of the noisiest ever in La Crosse" with children as well as adults setting off fireworks all night long. Accidents were numerous, but none were serious on this occasion. Other events of that day were harness races held at Neumeister's Osceola Park and large picnics on Indian Hill and at "the old shooting park" near South and West avenues.

Perhaps some got to see an entertainment spectacle that came to La Crosse on July 20 with a traveling show called "Paine's Last Days of Pompeii". It covered five acres, including an artificial lake containing gaily-lighted gondolas. The show featured Roman chariot races, stage acts, and a reproduction of the volcano Vesuvius erupting, as well as a grand display of fireworks of every conceivable design in water, on land, and in the sky. About 1,700 people turned out for the event at Green Bay Street and West Avenue.

Miss Sweeney, a teacher at La Crescent's Old Brick School in 1911 sits in a very tidy classroom. [LA CRESCENT AREA HISTORICAL SOCIETY ARCHIVES]

Or, they could have participated in a more intimate social gathering like the one that took place at Miss Margaret Marston's house at 324 West Avenue South, July 21 when she gave a bicycle tea party for her friends. The account said, "The boys and girls made quite a formidable procession as they gracefully wheeled along Cass Street, 30 or more being in the line. After the ride, they returned to the Marston house...for refreshments and dancing."

Some children may have had to part with their fathers for a while when several La Crosse firms were involved in the construction of new buildings at the State School for the Feeble Minded at Chippewa Falls, Wisconsin on July 24. Contractor Wooley had the general building contract; James Trane had the plumbing contract and Segelke & Kohlhaus furnished most of the mill fixtures.

Some may have had relatives affected by a report on July 25 that, "Some white livered scoundrel is poisoning chickens belonging to residents in the vicinity of 17th and Market streets. One man claims to have lost over 70 chickens to the poison fiend."

Families might also have been annoyed by travel as a July 28 news story commented: "After being torn up for two months and being the subject of much complaint, the Rose Street viaduct is being replanked and will soon be ready to accommodate the traveling public."

Maybe someone knew Archie Morse or Fred Clark, of La Crosse, who on August 8 swam from the Milwaukee Railroad drawbridge (same one still used today) to the wagon bridge, (forerunner of the Cass Street bridge) a distance of about 2 miles, in a time of 45 minutes.

Perhaps they got candy at the La Crosse Cracker and Candy Company on 208 S. Front Street, that was then busy making political novelty cakes in the shape of McKinley and Bryan on August 14. The likenesses of the presidential candidates were stamped on the top of the cakes.

Or maybe the kids were intrigued by a report from August 26, which stated, "Workers digging for a sewer on S. 7th Street, near South Avenue, come across several skeletons, thought to be those of Indians buried many years ago."

1896 may have been an interesting year for teachers reading "What I Did on My Summer Vacation".

Information from *La Crosse Time Trip 1896*, edited by Doug Connell, the *La Crosse Daily Press*, the *La Crosse Morning Chronicle*, the *La Crosse Republican & Leader* and the *Weekly Argus*, published in La Crosse during 1896.

CHAPTER 9:
THE GOOD OLD DAYS –
OR WERE THEY?

IT'S A WONDER ANYONE SURVIVED!
Epidemics of Houston County

Did you ever wonder about the many graves of small children in the old part of the cemeteries? In the mid-1800s medicine was still pretty primitive. In the 1850s the stethoscope was new and the clinical thermometer hadn't even been invented yet. Surgeons only washed their hands *after* surgery, not before. What caused most illnesses was still a mystery. It's no wonder so many children died.

This funeral procession was a Masonic Rite for the funeral of H.D. Gurley of La Crescent on April 27, 1915. The procession was on north Walnut Street in La Crescent between Main Street and 1st Street north. The Potter-Gittens house is in the background. The Gittens house has been designated as a historic home. [LA CRESCENT AREA HISTORICAL SOCIETY ARCHIVES]

There were a number of epidemics in Southeastern Minnesota in the 1800s according to local historian Anita Palmquist of the Houston County Historical Society. The diphtheria epidemic of 1874 claimed many children as victims as it swept through families in the area. Approximately 85% of deaths from diphtheria were among youngsters in the first five years of life. This disease, as well as cholera, often killed three or four children in a single family during an epidemic.

Diphtheria was an especially horrible disease, as described by the *Modern Home Medical Advisor*. It began with a sore throat, followed by a fever, damage to the heart, paralysis and a membrane that grew in the throat, until the victim could no longer swallow or breathe. In the 1874 epidemic, all a doctor could do to try to save a patient gasping for air, was to try to suck out the membrane or cut a hole in the throat for the victim to breathe.

Imagine in 1874, Mary, 8, the oldest of your five young children comes home from school and says she has a sore throat. At first you don't think much of it, especially before the disease is known in the area. "A cold", you think. You try to make sure she is dressed warm enough, and give her something warm to drink. Mary gets feverish. You send her to bed. Her throat seems to fill up. She tries to spit out the phlegm, but can't, as the membrane grows in her throat.

You dab her forehead and give her more water and hot soup. The child becomes weaker as the disease injures her heart. You can see she is getting worse. As the disease progresses, little Mary becomes paralyzed and eventually, she can't swallow the soup or even water anymore. Finally, poor little Mary is gasping for air as breathing becomes impossible. You call a doctor in desperation. After examining your little girl, the doctor tries to suck the membrane out, and cuts a hole in her windpipe to help her breathe. He looks at you compassionately, and tells you your daughter has diphtheria. There is nothing more to do. It's too late. There is no cure.

Dread fills you as you look at Katy, Anna, Seth and baby William, knowing how contagious the disease is. But for now, you concentrate on little Mary. You think, "Why, God? Why are you taking our little Mary from us? She has always been such a helpful child. Why can't she get well? Where did she get this terrible disease?"

Mary dies, and in the process of digging her grave in a nice spot on the farm, Seth tells you his "froat" hurts. The next day Anna says she has a sore throat and the baby won't be consoled. You hug them all, wishing that could keep them from the likely diagnosis. Katy, too, comes down with the symptoms. The fear and dread increase with the grief as you bury the baby and Seth. Anna, too dies. Katy has a hard time of it, but somehow eventually gets better in the midst of cries and pleas to God in your prayers.

The story repeats itself in one home after another in the community without regard to income, national origin or creed. Small graves and cemeteries spring up in favorite spots of the farms and near the churches. Funerals aren't allowed during the epidemic, in hopes of keeping the dreadful disease from spreading. People die all the same.

A few years later, cholera hits the community, and once again, the small children and the elderly are the first to die. A form of dysentery, the victims lose enormous amounts of liquids and minerals from their bodies, sending them into shock and death.

Doctors were a luxury on this side of the river in the early days of settlement and not readily obtainable. Dr. James P. Sheldon of Mound Prairie, who moved to the area in 1853, Dr. P.R. Kibbee and Dr. A.J. Carpenter of Hokah, or Dr. W.W. Holden of La Crosse, who were listed as area doctors in an 1886 Hokah Sun newspaper may have treated such diseases in the area.

In the early 1880s, germs are discovered to cause many diseases. Scientists find that a germ divides every 20 minutes. If a single germ divided and made 2 new ones every hour, at the end of the day it will have 16 ½ million descendants. Eventually, they find that people coming in contact with nearly anything the diseased person touched can spread diphtheria. A person who recovers from it, can still carry the disease in their systems for up to 10 months. Worse yet, people who once had it and recovered can carry it to others during an epidemic without ever knowing it.

Thankfully, anti-toxins were then discovered to immunize children from those most dreaded diseases. Now such diseases are nearly wiped out where children are immunized. The prevention of such diseases is considered one of the greatest contributions of modern medical science.

Dr. Louis K. Onsgard of Houston, from 1892 – 1919 likely dealt with a more recent epidemic that our most senior citizens might remember – the Spanish Influenza of 1918. It spread like wildfire during World War I across the entire world. Such a harsh flu was this that nearly half of the soldiers who died in that war died from the flu. It killed 20-40 million people worldwide. Of those, more than 500,000 were Americans. Often it turned into pneumonia, which killed many and was thought to later lead to Tuberculosis outbreaks. Area schools were ordered closed during the epidemic and events were cancelled to stem the spread of the disease.

An ad for a patent medicine in the November 21, 1918 Houston County Chief offered: "Quick Relief" for the flu. It said, "Don't wait until your cold develops Spanish Influenza or pneumonia. Kill it quick – Hill's Bromide Cascara Quinine".

In a December 5, 1918 issue of that paper, an article from the U.S. Public Health Service stated: "SPAIN AND ENGLAND REPORT INCREASE IN TUBERCULOSIS AFTER INFLUENZA EPIDEMIC. ...One Million Cases Tuberculosis In United States – Each a Source of Danger." It continued, "Influenza Convalescents Should Have Lungs Examined – Colds Which Hang On Often Beginning of Tuberculosis. No Cause for Alarm If Tuberculosis Is Recognized Early – Patent Medicines Not to Be Trusted."

These diseases still exist and have only been kept at bay with immunizations and modern medicine. In the case of such deadly diseases, an ounce of prevention is definitely worth a pound of cure.

Information from Anita Palmquist, *Modern Home Medical Advisor*, 1886 *Hokah Sun* and 1918 *Houston County Chief*.

WHERE HAVE ALL THE TREES GONE?

Saving Timber in 1876

These days we pat ourselves on the back for finally thinking about the environment and natural resources with our proclamation of "Earth Day". But such thought was evidenced more than 125 years ago in the *Congressional Record* of April 28, 1876.

It was a time of massive logging with much territorial lumber being sent down our own Mississippi River. Lumber uses were many and necessary in those days. For instance, according to the document, in 1871, 10,000 acres of forest were stripped of their timber to supply fuel for the single city of Chicago; and fences chiefly of wood, valued at $1.8 billion in the United States, were costing $98 million per year for repairs and renewal, not to mention lumber needs for building houses, businesses and furniture. A note was also made of "the constantly multiplying uses of wood, the result, in part, of inventions."

Still, one of the largest consumers of wood then was the railroad. The record stated: "To give 2,500 sleepers [*Note: railroad ties that support the rails of the train track*] to the mile these roads required 150,000,000 of trees, each tree making generally but one sleeper. These sleepers require renewal every five years, making a demand for 30,000,000 of trees per annum...Each engine with an ordinary train consumes about 1-¾ cords for every 25 miles. This gives an annual consumption of 6,500,000 cords of wood. The 60,000 miles of railway require, at the rate of 40 poles per mile, 2,400,000 trees. These also decay and will require renewal."

Later in the document, these overwhelming numbers were translated into areas affected by unchecked lumbering: "We have left untouched in the whole United States but one really fine tract of timber, consisting of about one-half of Washington Territory and a third of Oregon. California has perhaps 500,000 acres of fuel, one-half of which has been cut away within the last two years…"

The record continued in alarm: "New York has lost her maple, walnut and hickory and now has no considerable forest left, except what is to be found in her Adirondacks. The Wisconsin forests are in process of rapid destruction: no less than 1,030,000,000 trees have been cut in a single year. Tens of thousands of logs are rafted down the Mississippi to towns in Iowa, where they are cut into lumber… and your petitioner predicts that if the present destruction goes

The timber industry used sleds like this in the winter to move logs. The unidentified men drive their load past the Old Brick School in La Crescent in the early 1900s. [LA CRESCENT AREA HISTORICAL SOCIETY ARCHIVES]

on, in ten or twenty years at most not only the forests of Wisconsin, but Michigan and Minnesota will be swept away."

Author of this 1876 speech, Minnesota Representative Mark H. Dunnell, continued with consequences of losing timber without replacing it: "The summers are hotter and the winters colder. This can be referred to the destruction of the forests along the tributaries of the Mississippi…Temperature, moisture, climate and pestilence are all mastered in a degree by forests. Our changes in climate not only increase diseases, but produce new ones. The narrowing of the winter wheat belt and of the fruit zone so as to reduce their areas by millions of acres is also a result of these irregularities. The healing influence of the conifer upon those afflicted with consumption, catarrhal, asthmatic and throat difficulties is also an important count in the case at issue..."

Mr. Dunnell cited among others, the case of Valencia, in South America: It "was formerly situated about one mile and a half from a beautiful lake which was surrounded by a dense forest. The trees were cut away, and in the course of time the waters re-ceded to a distance of four and a half miles. The trees were afterward replaced by others, and in about twenty-two years the lake returned to its original boundaries...Many instances can be furnished where lands, once gardens of freshness, beauty and fertility have become utter deserts by the removal of the forests which covered them." He included examples of failing springs and streams in the eastern U.S. due to diminished forests.

To preserve forests and quality of life for future generations, Rep. Dunnell suggested a tree planting campaign to celebrate the centennial of the nation, studying schools of forestry, and establishing a "commissioner of forestry to prepare a yearly report, showing the annual consumption of lumber in the United States and the amount reproduced, the most suitable kind of trees to plant in each state, and their influence upon the climate, together with tables and statistics relative to the renewal of forests in foreign countries."

(Because of objection to the multiplication of federal offices, Rep. Dunnell emphasized that no new office would be created.) The amendment was agreed to. Thank you Representative Dunnell.

Information from the April 28, 1876 *Congressional Record*.

"IT WARN'T EASY BACK IN 1881"
Life in the Victorian Era

What was life like in 1881? For the well to do, it was a time of fancy clothes, bicycles (yes, bicycles), large houses and live entertainment. Although it was a simpler, slower-paced time, there were many inconveniences, even for the rich.

For instance, the large Victorian houses, luxurious as they might have been, had no bathrooms, since the flush toilet was not yet in use. Like everyone else, the rich had to use outhouses, and "chamber pots" for nighttime use and during bad weather. With no showers, they washed up with the large bowls and pitchers of water provided in the bedrooms.

A nice Victorian house in 1881 had, for instance, a kitchen, office, dining room, sitting room, parlor (where the family deceased were laid out for a wake in the days before funeral homes) and two porches on the first floor. The second floor might have a sewing room and four bedroom "chambers". The third floor was often finished as a ballroom for parties and dancing. A house like that made of brick and stone with wooden trim and a slate floor cost $6,500 to build in 1881.

Although it may have been furnished with the intricately carved ornate furniture of the period, that antique lovers are so fond of today, all the little nooks and crannies of the pieces were a real headache to dust and keep clean in the days of mostly wood and coal burning stoves. Carpets also were hard to clean, as they had to be thrown over the clothesline and hit repeatedly with a wire rug beater to shake the dust from them. Although anyone who could afford them, had maids to help with the work, as the cleaning was never ending in the large houses.

Food preparation was also a chore with no microwave ovens or pre-packaged food – unless it was canned in the harvest season.

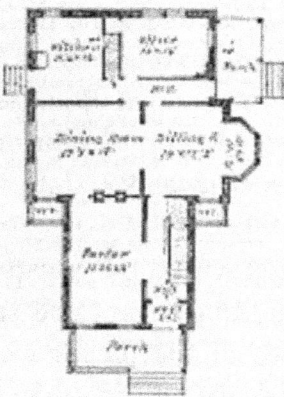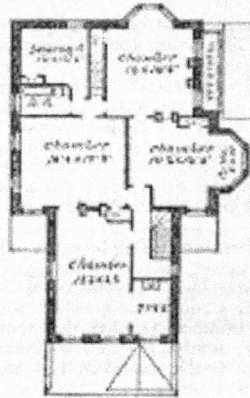

House plans of a Victorian home in 1881. Often times the top floor of the more palatial Victorian homes were used as ballrooms for house dances. [GODEY'S LADY'S BOOK AND MAGAZINE – 1881]

People often had to hunt for their meat, especially on the frontier. So they ate what was available, such as rabbit, squirrel, quail and pigeons, as well as fish and domestic meat like pork, beef and poultry. Much more of the animals were eaten, including the heads and feet. This was not considered gross, but practical. Fruits and vegetables were whatever was locally grown.

Without refrigerators, recipes used lots of eggs and butter to use them up before they spoiled. (A wedding cake, for instance, used 40 eggs!) Recipes had no cooking or baking temperature, since stoves typically fueled with wood had no temperature gauge. Measurements were by the pound, quart, coffee— or teacup, "pinch" or silverware teaspoon or tablespoon, or "to taste."

With no TV, radio or other recorded music, movies, Nintendo, computers, or automobiles, people entertained each other. They had "parlor games" which were often guessing games or might involve acting things out. They also had word puzzles and sang songs along with a piano or other musical instruments if they had them. People also visited each other, read books, went to plays, lectures, sporting events, community events and celebrations, and to dances in each other's homes.

Bicycles became very popular and people who rode them were known as "wheelmen." Many were in riding clubs. The bicycles were often made locally and varied in style. In 1881, the huge front wheels and small back wheels were popular for men. Women rode a more lady-like "tricycle" with a large wheel on either side, like a wheelchair, and a small wheel for balance in the back. Steering handles for the tricycles were often on either side instead of the front.

Women's apparel that we commonly see on the street these days would have been considered indecent – if not scandalous in 1881. At that time, women's dresses and skirts were always floor length and full. The ample dresses were laundered by hand, hung up

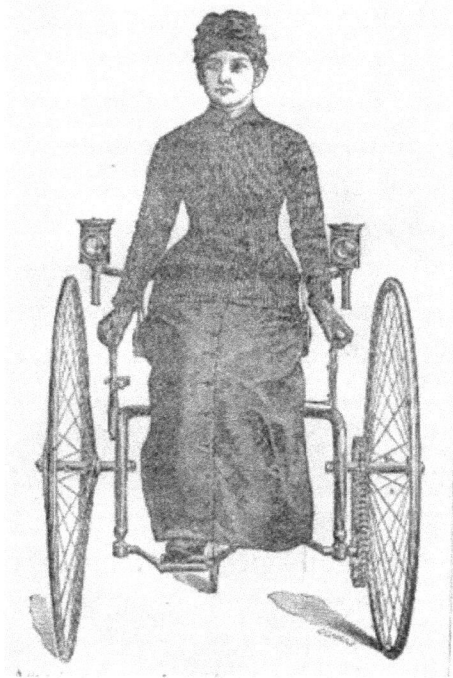

Bicycling was all the rage in the late 1800s. This version was created as a lady-like tricycle for women in 1881, so they could join in the fun. [GODEY'S LADY'S BOOK AND MAGAZINE – 1881]

to dry and were ironed with heavy "flat irons" that were heated on the stove. One frilly woman's dress may have taken an hour to iron. "Ladies" didn't wear pants except for certain physical activities like horseback riding or swimming that necessitated a full feminine version of them. Even the pants of women's swimsuits were below the knee in length, with skirts over them and could have long or short sleeves. The swimsuits were made of serge, flannel or wool.

Although we romanticize about what life was like in those Victorian days in the beautiful Victorian homes, I doubt many of us today would like to live the way they did.

Information from the 1881 *Godey's Lady's Magazine* (year's worth bound edition), the video, "The 1900 House" and a tour of President Grant's home in Galena, Illinois.

IT'S TOO DARN HOT!
Summertime 1881

Suppose it was a hot summer day in La Crescent around 125 years ago and you wanted to cool off. Of course, there was no such thing as air conditioning, or even electric fans. You could sit in the shade and fan yourself by hand. Or, if you were lucky, to perhaps cool your drink of water, you might use some precious ice chipped off a block of ice harvested from the Mississippi River during the winter and stored under sawdust in an icehouse. Maybe the water was already cool if just hand-pumped from a well. Otherwise it may have been getting warm from sitting since morning in a bucket with a dipper in it for everyone's use.

If the drink didn't work, there were no lawn sprinklers to run through or swimming pools to go to, but you might find a dip in a creek, pond or the Mississippi River refreshing. Of course, if you were swimming in the Mississippi in the latter half of the 19th Century, you had better watch out for logs being rafted down the river to saw mills, and for a variety of boats with people, supplies and livestock on board, traveling the busy river.

A lady going swimming in 1881 in proper attire might have worn a swimsuit similar to one shown in a picture, from the 1881 *Godey's Lady's Book and Magazine.*

One "bathing hat" was made of white linen, and bound and trimmed with about an inch wide band of navy blue cashmere, with a bow on top and at the back, and had an oil-silk cap attached, presumably to keep the hair dry. A bathing suit featured, was a mid-calf length gown with short sleeves made of blue flannel, trimmed with three or four rows of white braid accenting the sleeves, wide pointed collar and hemline. A blanket or "mantle" covering it was an early swimsuit cover-up, to be worn to and from the bathhouse and kept dry. It was made of a white woolen material bordered with a wide band of blue background material with white stripes on it. The

Bathing suit fashions of 1881. The swimsuits could be made of serge, flannel or wool and could be made with long or short sleeves. Men's and boys' swimsuits were not shown. [GODEY'S LADY'S BOOK AND MAGAZINE – 1881]

accompanying bathing hat was Oriental looking, made of straw, woven in a circular pattern to a peak on the top of the head, with the edges trimmed with small dangling pom-poms. All bathing hats had attached oil-silk caps.

The other swim apparel shown for a young lady was a two-piece suit. The knee-length over-dress was made of navy-blue serge (a lighter weight material of twilled silk or rayon used for suits or linings) and was trimmed with ruffled red braid at the bottom of the sleeves, wide pointed collar and hem. A sash, which tied in the front at the waist, was also red. The sort of mid-calf-length pants underneath, were referred to as "drawers". They were also trimmed with red ruffles at the bottom of the pants legs.

A notation was added, "These suits can all be made with long sleeves, but the short ones are better adapted to swimming." (A reminder not only of the fashion of the day, but also, that you couldn't order the swimsuits ready made. You could only order the pattern and then sew them yourself or have a seamstress sew them for you.) The hat accompanying that suit was sportier, with a more streamlined look, made of straw trimmed with red and blue woolen material draped across the crown and finished with a decorative knot in front. The book didn't say if you could order the hats, so presumably, you would show a milliner (hat maker) a picture of the hat and the milliner would make the hat for you.

A little girl's knee-length dress-like swimsuit pictured was made of pink serge trimmed with blue serge at the capped sleeves and collarless neckline. A blue scarf tied in the back, around the dropped waistline. Her hat was also of straw covered with a gathered piece of blue cotton and ribbon at the crown.

All of the models were sporting sandals – but even they were laced up for a high top look.

The little girl carried a sand shovel, which was probably metal, and possibly borrowed from the fireplace for some fun digging in the sand.

Swimming was a great way to cool off in the heat even back then – if you didn't drown from the heaviness of the wet clothes. The alternative was "skinny-dipping" if you could be sure no one else was around, and that Mother wouldn't find out.

Information from 1881 Godey's Lady's Book and Magazine and from general information about the La Crosse / La Crescent area of that time.

PASSING THE BUCKET

Firefighting a Century Ago

Volunteer fire departments still protect small communities from raging fires. In the early days of La Crescent, the firefighters had little training and included anyone big enough to pass a bucket of water. A newspaper account of the way it was in the late 1800s or early 1900s follows as written:

DISMISS SCHOOLS TO FIGHT FIRE
PUPILS IN BUCKET BRIGADE CALLED UPON
TO SAVE LA CRESCENT PROPERTY

Three hours of hard fighting saves adjoining property, but house of Ed Wheeler upon which insurance had expired but a few days ago damaged to extent of $200.

The school children of La Crescent released from school to assist the citizens in fighting the flames in bucket brigades yesterday saved La Crescent from a serious fire. As it was the conflagration burned furiously the home of Edward Wheeler and it was only after the hardest work that it was controlled.

At about 11 o'clock yesterday morning fire was discovered in the Wheeler residence in the attic. It is presumed that it caught from the stove pipe which ran through the apartment. Before it was seen it had gained great headway and it was evident at once that all of the help that could be commanded was necessary to save the home and perhaps, some in the immediate vicinity.

[Note: In the days before central heating, houses

often had stoves only on the first floor. A hole was cut in the ceiling above the stove for the stovepipe to pass through to the roof. Thus the upper floor also received some heat from the hot stovepipe.]

The alarm was given and the schools were released and the larger pupils were banded into three bucket brigades together with the men of the village and for three hours they dashed water upon the flames, pailful by pailful until it was extinguished.

The loss on the house will be $200 and a peculiar feature of the fire is that the insurance which had been carried for several years expired but a few days ago.

Because of terrible fires which destroyed many wooden frame buildings in downtowns in the early days of settlement, many communities implemented ordinances which mandated that businesses in close proximity to one another in the downtown areas be built of brick to keep the fires more easily contained and from burning down the whole downtown.

The inventions of water pumper trucks and fire hydrants to all the modern fire fighting equipment are indeed a blessing. They, and modern firefighting techniques have saved untold amounts of property and lives. Finally, most communities now have professionally trained firefighters, so they don't have to rely on students throwing water on destructive fires by the pailful.

Information from an undated, unidentified local news clipping and from *Echoes of the Past* by Myer Katz.

THE WAY-BACK MACHINE VISITS DECEMBER, 1898

Bits of News from 1898

Imagine if you could time-travel and see what the area was like a century ago. Maybe you spent that month in the more populated La Crosse, Wisconsin, directly across the Mississippi River from La Crescent, Minnesota. Would it be filled with the romance of a simpler time as we would like to think? Was life better then? What would we be able to witness in, say, December of 1898?

Well, on December 4, 1898 a person at 1102 Caledonia Street in La Crosse would have seen a sober scene of an overflow crowd, with people seated in the aisles, packing St. James Church, for a memorial mass honoring soldiers who died in the Spanish-American War. Out of respect to the memory of the dead, the church was draped in black and white along with an abundance of the stars and stripes.

December 13 of that year you may have seen the Galena House that once stood at 115 N. Front Street – a popular stopping place for river men for many year – sold to the Heileman Brewing Company. John Donaghoe, owner of the hotel and saloon business was one of the early settlers of La Crosse. He was retiring after selling his hotel.

On December 14 you might have heard hollers and screams as you witnessed a Streetcar colliding with a wagon carrying a load of slabs on the Causeway. The streetcar was heavily damaged in the crash. Fortunately, none of the passengers in the car were injured, though they were given a bad jolt and scare.

You may have had a feeling of déjà vu as you read in the newspaper of December 17 that for the third time, a Madison court ruled that Daniel Cameron, of La Crescent, Minnesota, was the lawful owner of the Cameron Park property in La Crosse. The City of La Crosse thinking it was the owner of the land due to early clerical errors in city records, planned to again appeal the decision. [*Note: La Crosse later was sold this parkland by Daniel Cameron's heirs. This same Cameron Park in the early 2000's is once again embroiled in multiple legal battles, this time, over the 10 Commandment monument placed there in 1965. The argument now is over separation of church and state.*]

That day, also if you wanted to cross the Mississippi River over James Vincent's wooden "ice bridge", located just south of Cass Street, you would have to pay a five cent toll for passage on a round trip.

Looking for sledding fun on December 20th, you might have gone to the aid of the 5-year-old son of Mr. And Mrs. Sidney Maine, 613 Rose Street, who suffered cuts and bruises when he collided with a tree while sledding down the Rose Street viaduct.

You might have heard of the dance on December 23, 1898. – Employees of the La Crosse Rubber Mills were given a dance in the new addition recently built to the factory on Indian Hill. The dance, attended by 150 couples, was appropriately named the "Rubber Ball".

December 24 may have found you surprised to see Santa Claus and his sleigh, pulled by an Eskimo dog! A large crowd of admiring small boys followed the rig sponsored by Doerflinger's Store as it traveled about the streets of La Crosse.

If you went to the Christmas program at the Norwegian Methodist Episcopal Church, 1454 Liberty Street in La Crosse on December 25, you would have been surprised by an unwelcome show of another kind. A well-known North side young man, under the influence of

A snowy winter scene from a Christmas postcard postmarked 1911. [LA CRESCENT AREA HISTORICAL SOCIETY ARCHIVES]

alcohol, attempted to disturb the program. His plans however, "were frustrated", and he was sent home with a black eye.

December 26th may have found you touched by the generosity of J. E. Willing who gave away 300 bags of candy and popcorn to children who called at his clothing and shoe store, 115 S. 4th Street. On Christmas Day Willing gave away 120 chickens to the poor of the city for use in Christmas dinners.

If you competed in the roller skating race at the Empire Rink, 412 S. 10th Street on December 31st, you likely would have been beaten by Helmus Peterson who won the six-day roller skating race. He covered 185 miles during 12 hours of skating over six days. Kero Colby placed second with 182 miles.

The leading social event of New Year's Eve was the Sylvester Ball presented by the Deutscher Verin at Germania Hall, 720 5th Avenue

South in La Crosse. If you were lucky enough to attend, you would have found decorations of red, green and white, with attendees being impressed with the place being brilliantly lighted with a myriad of electric lights. The musicians were seated on the stage and were partly hidden by palms and ferns. You would have danced in the New Year with "the cream of La Crosse society" at the time.

So, with the month of December, 1898 over, would you be ready to return to the present? Overall, it wasn't a bad time or place for a time-travel visit.

Information from *La Crosse Time Trip 1898* edited by Doug Connell of bits of news gleaned from area newspapers of the time.

FOLK REMEDIES WITH GOOSE GREASE AND MUSKRAT SKINS

Doctoring Without a Doctor

Until the technological age, medical treatment was scarce in newly settled areas and not very scientific. People rarely sought out a doctor unless they thought they or someone else was in danger of dying. They figured out basic first aid and home remedies for common ailments by trial and error that were effective to various degrees. And if the remedy worked, they likely didn't know how or why – it just did.

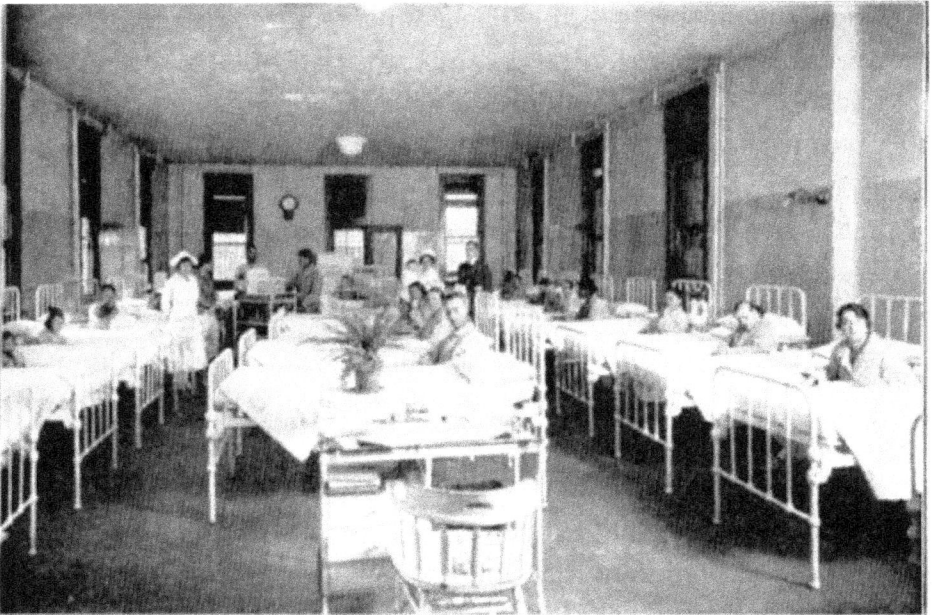

Hospital privacy has come a long way since this photo of a hospital ward in the 1920s. [OURSELVES AND OUR CITY – 1928 SCHOOL TEXTBOOK]

The following are folk remedies garnered from the senior citizens of Dysart, Iowa by the area sixth graders in their 1994 book, *Ties That Bind*. Remember, these are remedies used when no doctors were available and are not recommended by the Historical Society to replace professional medical attention.

- To cure a sore throat, wrap a sock around your neck.
- To cure an earache, blow smoke in the ear. (Mother would then be sick for two days from smoking the cigar.)
- To cure a chest cold, mix goose grease with a little bit of turpentine and rub it on the chest and cover with a piece of flannel cloth.
- For a really stubborn chest cold, make a mustard plaster by mixing equal amounts of powdered mustard and flour with warm water to make a paste. Spread between two pieces of muslin and apply to chest. Be careful not to leave it on too long, as it will burn the skin. For young children, prepared table mustard can be used so the mixture will not be so strong. A mustard plaster is good for curing a chest cold, pneumonia, and sore muscles.
- To cure coughing during the night, place a cold wet cloth on your neck, covered by a dry cloth; or boil an onion and use the juice as cough syrup.
- To protect yourself from scarlet fever, measles, or infantile paralysis, place a piece of asafetida (an ill-smelling plant gum) in a little cloth bag and pin it to your clothing. This keeps germs (and most people) away.
- Burn sulfur on the stove to keep the family from catching the flu
- To cure a baby's colic, drop five drops of anise seed oil and two of peppermint on half-ounce lump of sugar. Grind to a fine powder and give a little in water.
- To open a boil, place the white of an egg on the boil and cover it with a cloth. It will open all by itself. Another remedy for a boil is

to cover it with moistened dark bread and cover with a bandage.

- To ensure good health or for relief of warts, ulcers, eye irritations, growth of hair on head, to soften corns, or to thicken eyelashes, take one teaspoon of cod liver oil (nasty tasting stuff!)
- To cure a stomachache, make catnip tea by brewing a handful of catnip to one pint of water, sugar to taste.
- To control the bleeding from a cut, wrap the cut in brown wrapping paper.
- To draw out a sliver, wrap with a slice of raw potato.
- If you step on a nail, soak bread in milk and put it over wound to draw out infection.
- To cure a nosebleed, crowd the fingers tight into the ears and chew, pressing the teeth well together.
- To cure sprains, bruises, and rheumatism, place four newly laid eggs and one pint of the strongest vinegar you can find in a bottle and shake well. Then add two ounces of spirits of camphor and two ounces of turpentine. Shake well. Apply to problem area.
- To cure worms, put turpentine on a sugar cube and eat it.
- To be safe from lightning during a thunderstorm, sit on a feather pillow.
- To restore someone from a stroke of lightning, shower with cold water for two hours. If the patient does not show signs of life, put salt in the water and continue to shower an hour longer.
- Sufferers from asthma should get a muskrat skin and wear it over their lungs with the fur side next to the body. It will bring certain relief.
- Sulfur and molasses are used as a spring tonic to purify the blood.

Perhaps the new ways are better.

Information from *Ties That Bind* by Dysart, Iowa sixth-graders, 1994.

CHAPTER 10:
THE WINNER IS...

THE SNAKEBITE VOTE
A Voter's Dilemma in 1853

Politicians have tried wheeling and dealing for centuries, trying to get the votes of the masses for their desired position. Perhaps voters of past ages, as now, have been weary of politicians' promises. But one thing is certain: actions speak louder than words; and deeds done by those running for office are remembered much longer than their words.

Such an example comes from a family story in the 1919 *History of Houston County*. In 1853 Johannes Tuininga, a native of Holland, came to settle in the Pine Creek area west of La Crescent with his family. The following is the account, as written, of his story of crises and the politician who helped him:

Johannes Tuininga "...proved a permanent settler and was still living there in the early eighties. [*Note: 1880's*] At an early day, when physicians were scarce on the west side of the river, his wife was bitten by a rattlesnake. Having no money, he supposed it impossible to procure a physician, and so, in considerable agitation, he proceeded to apply the only domestic remedy of which he had heard. With a ton and a half of hay he had bought four fowls, and had raised 24 chickens. These he killed one after another, and laying them open, applied them in turn to the bitten part, but without any alleviation of the symptoms. While the family was in despair, a stranger was seen coming up the road. He was informed of the emergency and asked if he were not a physician, though Mr. Tuininga, honestly enough, told him beforehand that he had no money to pay one. The gentleman, who was H.M. Rice, of St. Paul, was not a physician, but he gave Mr. Tuininga $10 and told him to go for one at once. The doctor arrived and Mrs. Tuininga recovered. Mr. Tuininga never forgot this act of kindness, and when, years afterward, he saw Mr. Rice's name on a ticket at the polls for Governor, he voted the straight ticket of that party for the only time in his life."

Perhaps it's a lesson for all of us, politician or not, that kindness is never forgotten.

Information from the 1919 *History of Houston County*.

GRIDLOCK!
Vicious Politics in 1884

"Gridlock". Congressmen and senators keep bickering and nothing gets done. We wonder why can't they work together for the good of the country, like they're supposed to?

Let's look back in history via an 1884 Republican political flyer for Blain and Logan and see how it was then. It states:

> In 1882 the Democratic Party made hundreds of promises to voters, pledging themselves for changes in laws and for the enactment of new ones, provided they were given the House of Representatives. They were given a trial.
>
> The country gave them a *majority of seventy votes* in the House of Representatives...
>
> For more than *seven months* they were in session, and having been elected upon the sole issue of reform and retrenchment [*Note: a reduction of expenses*] let us inquire; *what* did they reform?
>
> Did they readjust the inequalities of the tariff law? No!
> Did they pass a bill to lessen the revenues? No!
> Did they remit any taxes? No!
> Did they pass a Naval Appropriation Bill? No!
> WHAT A REPUBLICAN SENATE DID!
> The Senate, being Republican, passed most of the above bills, but they were *strangled in a Democratic House*.

WHY SHOULD THEY NOW BE GIVEN POWER?

What legislation have they effected during the last seven months that should entitle them to further confidences of the voters of this country?

Answer – They passed the Fitz John Porter bill, which the President vetoed; they repealed the 'iron clad oath'; they partially paralyzed the industries of the country by a senseless agitation of the tariff question, and *they introduced a bill to repeal Civil Service Reform!*

What else did they do? They – adjourned!!! Thank God; adjourned!…

The *New York Herald* (Democratic) of July 8th enumerates the above measures and says:

'These and a few other acts of no great consequence, with a mass of minor enactments of little public concern, make up the list they have put through!

THE OTHER SUBJECT PROMISED IN 1882 WAS RETRENCHMENT.

Wherein did they retrench? Did the present Democratic House retrench?

ANSWER – They spent *Twenty Millions of dollars more than their Republican predecessors* in 1881…"

Throughout the years, we've seen the Republican Party just as guilty of the things listed as the Democratic Party. Maybe things haven't changed as much as we thought!

Information from 1884 political flyer.

CHAPTER 11:
BROTHER AGAINST BROTHER

HECK NO, I WILT NOT GO!
Civil War Protesters of Houston County

When we think about the Civil War, we rarely think of war protesters. Yet, they were a reality then, as perhaps in every war. The war protesters of Houston County were mainly immigrants, who had fled their countries for various reasons, including starvation and poverty. It's a hard thing to leave family, friends and all you know for an unknown place where everything is different, including the language. Many came here out of desperation, figuring it couldn't be worse here...but they didn't count on a war that had nothing to do with them.

By 1861 Houston County was already well settled. (La Crescent was founded in 1851 and settlement of the county continued.) Settlers came to this part of Minnesota across Wisconsin, crossing the Mississippi River at La Crosse, or many immigrants came up the Mississippi River and disembarked at Brownsville. The "Yankees" that settled here from the East came from New York, Connecticut, Pennsylvania and Ohio. Many of them had patriotic first names, such as "George Washington". Over all, they were financially better off than the immigrants, who were mainly German, Irish, Norwegian, Swedes and Scots.

The Germans and Irish settled in the southeast part of the county. Other Irish and the Scots settled in the southwest part of the county. Swedes settled in the Houston area. Settlement was often by ethnic groups so the immigrants would at least know the language and cultural customs in their local area. This area was also influenced by politics in La Crosse, just across the Mississippi River, which was at that time the forth-largest city in Wisconsin.

Then Governor Ramsey of Minnesota was a friend of President Lincoln when the Civil War broke out. He was first to offer troops to fight in the tragic war after the firing on Fort Sumter on April 12, 1861 by the Confederates. These first troops were the famed Minnesota 1st Regiment, which had three units from the Twin Cities, Hastings and Wabasha. They sustained a horrific loss of life in the first battles of the Civil War when all the men were "green" in battles that resembled "slug-fests" more than battles. Often times, soldiers didn't even know where the front lines were. (Because of the smoke from the guns and artillery, it was often hard to see in the battles, so the soldiers would have to listen for the sound of their bugler to know where the front line was.)

Houston County was mainly Democratic, in opposition to Governor Ramsey. Among these were a group of German settlers called "48-ers" that were vehemently opposed to the Civil War. Their point of view was reflected in the *Plain Dealer*, the La Crescent newspaper at the time. It was run by E.H. Purdy from the Twin Cities. He was a Democrat and severely anti-war. The *Hokah Chief*, which was a Republican newspaper, put pressure on him until he left. J.T. Ferguson bought the paper and ran it until it shut down when he served in the war. The next paper was called the *La Crescent Banner* and it remained a Democratic newspaper. It was sold to Rick Pomeroy of La Crosse, who was known as an outrageous mudslinger. He had seen Northern officers stealing from the South and was very bitter. He became nationally known as President Lincoln's worst enemy.

The immigrants of Houston County were only in this new country a short time and already, they were asked to fight in a war not of their making. Many resisted the Provost Marshall's first three draft calls. Eventually, some immigrants of Houston County decided they

Unidentified Houston County Civil War soldier of the Minnesota 10th Regiment, Company F 1862-1865. [LA CRESCENT AREA HISTORICAL SOCIETY ARCHIVES]

had to join the Union effort to keep the country together and preserve Democracy that was so dear to them after not having the benefit of it in the European countries they left. But in defiance to Governor Ramsey, they enlisted in Wisconsin, Iowa, Illinois, and even as far away as Missouri, Nebraska and Michigan, rather than in Minnesota.

Some of the young men who enlisted did so from ignorance of what war was really all about, as they sought adventure, wanting to leave the boredom of being isolated on farms where they rarely saw other people. Others just didn't want to do all the necessary hard work of farming. Badger Valley alone sent more than 30 young men to war, depopulating it of nearly all its young men.

The chaotic battle of Shiloh with 17,000 casualties was a wake-up call to the people back home when the letters of their loved ones came telling of the awful horrors of the unorganized battle. After that, enlistments dropped off. In 1864 there was a major migration of people from Houston County. Many, especially German immigrants, headed for the Idaho Territory that was not involved in the Civil War. Soldiers escorted the 120 wagons there for fear of the Indians, after the Sioux Uprising just two years earlier. At that time, the *Hokah Chief* also reported 69 draft dodgers. One man even went back to Germany to avoid the draft. Desertion was also a major problem of both the North and the South during the Civil War.

Charles Sea and Henrick Gluck of Brownsville, and a Mr. McDonald from Hokah, who were all railroad men for the Root River Railroad, were in charge of the draft of local soldiers. Of these men, Charles Sea became the Provost Marshall. Initially, enlistment was for a 90-day period, as had been the law at the start of the Civil War. But as more experienced men were needed to fight, the enlistment time became 3 years.

Although Minnesota ranked 7th from 37 states and seven territories with 14.7% of the population joining in the war effort, at that time Houston County was 600 men behind other areas in enlistments. The county was told to come up with 300 men in 20 days. But, this was no easy task.

At first, a man could pay another man $300 to go to war in his place. Later, according to La Crescent Township records from 1865, a special meeting was called to address the issue of enlistment for the Union on Feb. 8th of that year. It was noted:

> Whereas the President of the United States did in the 19th day of December 1864 order a draft for 300,000 men unless such number should be raised within 60 days by volunteering, of which number the township of La Crescent is required to fill its quota; and whereas future calls may be made by the President for volunteers; And whereas further it is believed that such quotas cannot be filled unless a town Bounty of at least $200 for each volunteer be authorized by the township. Therefore we the undersigned town officers and freeholders of the said town being desirous that the town should escape a draft deem it necessary to the interests of the town that a Special town meeting be called for the purpose of authorizing a township bounty of $200.00 for each volunteer who shall enlist and be credited to the town of La Crescent on the pending and all future drafts.

Finally, the county had to resort to throwing men in jail if they refused to answer the draft. The ages of the enlistees were from 18-45, with an average age of 37 in Houston County. Most men had the additional hardship of leaving their families behind in the new country to fend for themselves as they struggled to start farms or other businesses.

Because of the hardship of families in newly settled areas trying to harvest crops, farmers were allowed a leave of absence from the war to go home and help with the harvesting. While some Houston

County soldiers were home to do that, the Sioux Uprising occurred and many were called in an emergency situation to fight the Sioux Indians who were killing settlers in Minnesota in 1862. Of these, 5 died in the Sioux Uprising, but only one of these was killed in battle, and only three are buried in Houston County.

Samuel McPhail, the founder of Caledonia, was in charge of organizing a Union infantry of at least 70 men from Houston County. He had been an officer in the Mexican American War and was previously from Louisiana, so he knew the South. Colonel McPhail organized an infantry unit composed of 200 men, many from Wisconsin, Illinois, Iowa and Missouri and was in charge of the mounted cavalry, Company A – a company of honor. Fifty members of this company were from Houston County. Company K was also from Houston County.

Bull Run was the first Civil War battle for many of the Houston County men. Houston County suffered 77 casualties during the Civil War. Some of the area soldiers were captured by the Confederate Rebels and spent time at the Andersonville prisoner of war camp, where conditions were so terrible that 105-110 prisoners died per day ...many of starvation. (Often the only food they had was the entrails of slaughtered animals.) Of those who survived the Andersonville camp, some died later as a result of their wrecked health there.

Nearly all of the soldiers (95% of the Confederate soldiers and at least 55% of the Union soldiers) suffered the rest of their lives from amebic dysentery from drinking polluted water during the war. For this they received a government pension of $25 a year. Many of the veterans who returned from the Civil War were disabled and had limited futures. Many died not long after the war. John Ingman of the 8th Missouri was an example. He developed gangrene in his leg and foot, which had to be amputated. He received an $8 a month pension from the government for his disability. He employed himself then as a schoolteacher until his death.

The end of the war brought tears of sorrow for many who lost their loved ones in the war and tears of joy for those who saw their loved ones return. Still, the most heard comment of people who had their soldiers return after the war was: "He's just not the same."

As if the Civil War and Sioux Uprising didn't cause enough hardship, when the soldiers returned, a wall of water from a flood in 1866 rushed through the Root River Valley, killing more than 150 people.

If the Civil War protestors who left La Crescent for Idaho heard news from the La Crescent area, they surely must have thought this area was cursed at that time!

Information from a speech by David Klinski, a local historian from Caledonia who specializes in Civil War history, at the La Crescent Area Historical Society annual dinner   April 7, 2000 and from the La Crescent Township records of 1864-65.

CHILDREN OF THE BATTELFIED

A poem from the Civil War

Even as soldiers fought for freedom and their lives in the Civil War, their thoughts turned homeward and to family, the other victims of war. A fifth grade reading book (*Sanders' Union Fifth Reader*) from 1872 paid tribute to the battle of Gettysburg in a poem entitled: "The Children of the Battlefield," recounting this very concept.

Its touching stanzas received the prize offered by the Philadelphia Christian Commission for a poem on the death of Sergeant Humiston, of Portville, NY, who was found dead at Gettysburg several days after the battle, with his eyes fixed upon the ambrotype of his three children. The poem follows.

THE CHILDREN OF THE BATTLEFIELD
By James G. Clark

Upon the field of Gettysburg
The summer sun was high,
When Freedom met her haughty foe,
Beneath the Northern sky;
Among the heroes of the North,
Who swelled her grand array,
And rushed, like mountain eagles forth,
From happy home away,
There stood a *man* of humble name,
A sire of children three,
And gazed within a little frame,
Their pictured forms to see;
And blame him not, if in the strife
He breathed a soldier's prayer: –
"Oh, Father! Guard the soldier's wife,
And for his children care!"

Upon the field of Gettysburg
When morning shone again,
The crimson cloud of battle burst
In streams of fiery rain;
Our legions quelled the awful flood
Of shot, steel, and shell,
While banners, marked the ball and blood,
Around them rose and fell;
And none more nobly won the name
Of Champion for the Free
Than *he* who pressed the little frame
That held his children three;
And none were braver in the strife
Than he who breathed the prayer: --
"Oh, Father! Guard the soldier's wife,
And for his children care!"

Upon the field of Gettysburg
The full moon slowly rose;
She looked and saw ten thousand brows
All pale in death's repose;
And, down beside a silver stream,
From other forms away,
Calm as a warrior in a dream
Our fallen comrade lay;
His limbs were cold, his sightless eyes
Were fixed upon the three;
Sweet stars that rose in memory's skies
To light him o'er death's sea.
Then *honored* be the soldier's prayer: --
"Oh, Father! Guard the soldier's wife,
And for his children care!"

The reasons for wars and the technology of them may change, but the heartache and sorrow connected with them are still the same.

Information from 1872 *Sander's Fifth Union Reader*.

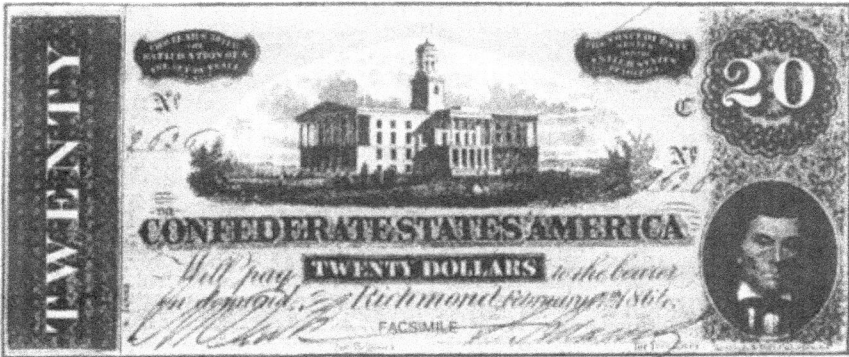

The Tennessee State Capitol Building at Nashville and Confederate Vice President, Alexander H. Stevens are featured on this replica Confederate $20 bill. Checking accounts were first used during the Civil War due to so much counterfeiting of currency. [COURTESY OF DONNA HUEGEL]

NEW MEANING TO "OLD MONEY"

Civil War Currency

Somehow, we tend to think that our money has always been issued by the Federal Government and has always looked the same. Of course, this is not true. Bartering of goods, like "my butter for your shoes", was common, as the United States seemed to be continually changing its boundaries. Gold and silver coins were accepted widely, but many towns created their own paper currency, as well, for trade in their own towns. Not until it became necessary to finance the Civil War did the United States have a national currency. Before then, individual banks issued their own paper money. (There were about 1,500 banks in 1862.) The North had its own money, and the South had different money. Much of the

Confederate money featured portraits of Civil War cabinet members and officers of the South.

During the Civil War, about half of the money was counterfeited. The solution to this problem was the introduction of bank checking accounts.

The gold value of Confederate money dropped from 90 cents on a dollar in 1861 to 1.7 cents at the end of the war, in 1865... approximately, the value of the paper it was printed on. Because of rampant inflation in the South, in 1864 butter cost $15 a pound and shoes cost $125 a pair.

People who have lived through times of war say that in war torn areas money is worth nothing, and people once again resort to bartering.

Information from souvenir replica currency of the Civil War from President Lincoln's home site in Springfield, Illinois and civilian survivors of Europe in World War II.

RUN FOR YOUR LIVES!

The Sioux Uprising

The timing couldn't have been worse for the settlers of Minnesota and the Dakotas when the Sioux Indians went on the warpath during the Civil War. It must have seemed like everyone was at war, and there was no safe place to live.

The Sioux Uprising was a backlash by the Sioux Indians in the beginning of August 1862 from being pushed out of their lands as the settlement West of the Mississippi River continued. (The Indians had been moved out of southeastern Minnesota in the 1840s.) The Sioux tribe, led by "Little Crow" went on a rampage that killed an undetermined number of settlers (estimates range from 800 to 2,000) in northern and western Minnesota and the Dakotas over a period of just over 40 days.

The uprising caught Minnesota off guard militarily as men in the Minnesota militia were away fighting in the Civil War at that time. Minnesota governor, Alexander Ramsey called back some of the troops fighting Confederate soldiers to fight the Indians at home.

The Iowa 27th and Wisconsin 25th troops were sent to put down the Indian rebellion. Both troops consisted of some men from Southeast Minnesota who joined the Union Army in those states. Five local men perished during the short-lived war, but only Captain John S. Cady of La Crescent who was captain of the Minnesota 8th was killed in the actual fighting with the Indians in 1862. The Grand Army of the Republic organization in La Crescent, which was a precursor of the VFW, was named after Captain Cady.

Some area farmers, who were granted a leave of absence from the Civil War to come home and harvest their wheat, were also immediately sent to help put down the uprising. They were sent to Fort Snelling in St. Paul and dispatched from there.

Generals Sibley and Sully of the Iowa 5th and 6th cavalry headed the group of militia sent to stop the Indian rebellion. By September, Sibley's troops numbered about sixteen hundred men eager to face half as many Sioux. About two thousand Indians were rounded up and driven into stockades at Mankato, Minnesota. Many of this number were women and children. In South Dakota the troops massacred 132 Indians – men, women and children – but many of these had no part in the Sioux Uprising. The legacy of Little Crow ended when a settler, who didn't know it was Little Crow, shot him as he was picking berries near Hutchinson, Minnesota.

Following this uprising many other settlers of western Minnesota (many were German immigrants) left the area in fear and did not return, which depopulated the white settlement of that area for a time.

This event caused the immigrants and settlers all over Minnesota to be paranoid about the Indians. According to David Klinski, a Civil War historian from Caledonia, Minnesota, local residents of the time panicked when a man from Spring Grove, Minnesota rode his horse through the town of Caledonia warning citizens that the Indians were coming! The settlers, being mainly Germans who owned no guns, fled en masse to Brownsville after releasing their livestock to fend for themselves. When it was learned that there was no Indian invasion on the way, the settlers returned to their homes to round up their scattered livestock, and some to find their homes had been robbed in their absence.

Such rumors even spread across the whole state of Wisconsin, panicking settlers to the point when Wisconsin's governor was ready to issue troops to defend the white population. This was known as the "Indian Scare of 1862".

I remember my grandmother, Hulda Christoph, who had been a German immigrant child in North Dakota and Minnesota in the late 1800s saying how afraid they were of Indians who came to their homestead. By that time, the Indians were defeated and destitute, coming around to beg for food, as they had nothing. (Entire herds of buffalo which had roamed the area and on which the Indians depended for food, clothing and shelter were slaughtered following the Sioux Uprising of 1862 for no other reason except to deprive the Indians of them. Some officials of the federal government went on record saying, "Indians could best be forced to accept 'civilization' by exterminating the bison.")

The stories of the Sioux Uprising a generation earlier were repeated to the new settlers from the few earlier settlers who had lived through it and stayed. The stories stuck in my Grandma's mind and I think she remained a bit afraid of Indians until she died in 1987 at the age of 94.

Information from a speech by David Klinski to the La Crescent Area Historical Society, April 7, 2000, *A Treasury of Minnesota Tales* by Webb Garrison and from stories from the author's grandmother, Hulda Christoph.

CHAPTER 12:
WARS TO END ALL WARS

NECESSITY IS THE
MOTHER OF INVENTION
World War I – War Changes Everything!

World War I changed the world forever. Not so much in geographical borders as by attitudes and technology. When the war broke out on July 28, 1914, the fashion of the day was still hats and floor-length dresses for women, and suits and hats for men at any social occasion. The role of married women was to tend to the home and raise the children. Women did not yet have the right to vote.

Because the war left a manpower shortage, and women were not expected or allowed to work outside the home, it was the black men who replaced the white workers in factories and such. Companies even created separate small apartment buildings for them to live in near the factories. The black men did not fight in the ranks yet, but did serve the other American soldiers their food.

German immigrants to the U.S. were fairly well established in their new communities and were proud of their heritage and the things their culture had brought to the new country; among them, breweries, wood carving skills, advances in agriculture, dance halls and gymnasiums. They started the concept of kindergarten in American schools. But once the war was underway, people of German heritage were under at least verbal attack in this country, as other groups somehow held them as responsible for the war as Germany itself. Thus, streets named after German cities were changed, and even "sauerkraut" was called "liberty cabbage" to eliminate an association with Germany.

This was the first "World War" with at least 28 countries involved in the fighting, with almost everyone lined up against Germany, which was looking for an excuse to take over more territory. Even countries not thought of as military powers enlisted in the fight – countries like Montenegro, New Zealand, India, Cuba, Panama, and Liberia. All were fighting because of the incident in Sarajevo, Bosnia where the Austrian Archduke, Franz Ferdinand was assassinated and Germany came to its defense.

It was a time when much of the world was ruled by kings and queens rather than by democracy. The world leaders at the time were invariably old men.

The war itself was an odd mix of the old and new. Mules and horses were still employed to move goods. But the "autotruck" soon found its new niche in hauling supplies more efficiently than could animals. Motorcycles and sidecars were also used, as well as skis and sleds in winter snow. There were warships, destroyers, submarines, torpedoes and mines.

A docked blimp in World War I. Flight and camouflage were new aspects of war introduced in World War I. [COLLIER'S NEW PHOTOGRAPHIC HISTORY OF THE WORLD'S WAR – 1919 BY P. F. COLLIER & SON]

Something new came into use in this war, however – flight. Balloons and dirigibles were used to spot enemy movements on both sides. Thus, was born the "new military science of camouflage" to hide from the enemy. The "aero planes" came to be used as a tool of war. The "monoplanes" (single wing planes) were left undeveloped in favor of the "biplanes" with two wings, which were thought to be more stable and better technology at the time.

(Left) Soldiers of World War I dressed in gas masks and armed with deadly gas canisters. Gas attacks were another first in war during World War I. (Right) World War I also introduced tanks to warfare. This one is a British model. Later, it dispensed with the rear wheel, as they found it was unnecessary. [COLLIER'S NEW PHOTOGRAPHIC HISTORY OF THE WORLD'S WAR – 1919 BY P.F. COLLIER & SON]

Machine guns and "colossal guns" (huge artillery) the size of which had never been seen before were used. The "tank" was introduced, as was the use of poisonous gas for warfare. Man's ingenuity had created more deadly and efficient ways to destroy property, nature and one another.

War changes the world in many different ways. The Armistice (end) of that war is celebrated on Nov. 11 – Veteran's Day. It was called "The War to End All Wars". If only it had been!

Information from *Collier's New Photographic History of the World's War* by Francis J. Reynolds and C.W. Taylor, And from *The United States in World War I* by Don Lawson

WAITING FOR NEWS

World War II News Aboard the U.S.S. Yorktown

There was a time when World War II was not history but news.

The following are excerpts of the news accounts sailors on the U.S.S. Yorktown received via Radio Press News during WW II while in the Pacific Ocean:

Feb. 26, 1945.

"...On Iwo the leathernecks beat off attacks on both flanks as they inched toward the central airfield. To the south where Old Glory flies atop Mount Suribachi, the Marines were using flamethrowers and explosives against enemy caves, pillboxes and crevices on the steep sides of the extinct volcano. It was man-to-man fight on the mountain slopes. In their fight for Iwo's number two airstrip, the Marines face a maze of enemy gun positions. The silencing of Jap batteries atop the volcano lessened the threat to supply lines. American warships continued their round-the-clock blasting of Iwo. Swarms of carrier planes joined in the attack. Marine casualties were running high. During the first fifty-seven hours of fighting, 644 were killed, 4,168 wounded and 560 missing. Japanese dead actually counted totaled 1,222 and indications were that Nippon losses were much heavier. Marine Lt. General Holland M. Smith, directing the leathernecks at Iwo, said 'Our fanatical enemy will fight to the bitter end. It must not be forgotten that the Japs consider Iwo a part of their homeland.' He added, 'The enemy has wrecked many boats, LST's [*Note: Landing Ship Tanks*] and ducks but sufficient rations, water and ammunition have been landed to carry on the battle...'"

April 10, 1945.

"...The U.S. Third Army struck a tottering Reich a resounding economic blow yesterday by capturing Germany's 'Fort Knox' bullion and millions in currency and art treasures in a day that saw the enemy reel under fresh battle disasters. Lt. Gen. Patton's soldiers captured an old salt mine in Thuringia and twenty one hundred feet underground discovered the vault in which the wealth was stored. The vault contained one hundred tons of gold bullion... In addition, a huge store of currency totaling millions of dollars was found including two million American dollars, three billion marks, 100 million French francs, 110 thousand British pounds, four million Norwegian crowns and lesser amount of Turkish pounds, Spanish pesetas and Portuguese escudos. Taken along with this store were three officials of the Reichsbank. One official said the bullion was all the gold in Germany. The Germans were said to be trying desperately to move the hoard, but wrecked transportation and bridges slowed their efforts and the Americans got there first..."

Somehow, history seems a little more real and interesting when we read it as it happened, -- when it was "news".

An American ship in the Pacific Ocean blasts its 16-inch guns during fighting in World War II. [BUREAU OF NAVAL PERSONNEL INFORMATION BULLETIN – NOVEMBER, 1944 – MAGAZINE FOR ALL HANDS]

Information from memorabilia donated to the La Crescent Historical Society by the Donald Frappier family.

THE "BOMB"

The World is Introduced to the Atomic Age

World War II was coming to a close. The war was over in Europe, but the Japanese were still fighting fiercely. Even as more troop ships were heading for the South Seas, President Truman made the decision to use our ultimate weapon: the atomic bomb, in hopes of shortening or ending the war in the Pacific. The following are accounts of the war news about the dropping of the atomic bombs on Japan as received by sailors on the U.S.S. Yorktown in the Pacific Theater of the war:

Saturday, 11 August, 1945

GUAM: "...The second enemy city to feel the fantastic power of the new atomic bomb took its explosive beating about noon Thursday, Japanese time. It was the big Kyushu seaport of Nagasaki. General Carl Spaatz Chief of Strategic Air Forces says the bombing achieved good results, but photos taken by reconnaissance planes three hours after the vast explosion showed smoke still rising to 20,000 feet and the city itself obscured so that observation was impossible. Therefore, full details are not yet known. The United Press says, however, it is almost certain that the atomic bomb scored heavily again after Monday's initial attack which devastated Hiroshima. Only silence came from Japan concerning the fate of Nagasaki, though she claimed through her commentators that 'The Allies are far behind the scientific times in regards to the atomic bomb development', and said the principle of the bomb was undoubtedly stolen from the Japanese government..."

WASHINGTON ROUNDUP

WASHINGTON: "President Truman told the American people today that only surrender will stop the use of the new and terrible atomic bomb. Speaking in his first lengthy address to the nation since becoming the Chief Executive, Mr. Truman gave no direct indication as to when that surrender might come. But he said the Soviet decision to declare war on Japan was only one of the secret military arrangements made at the Potsdam Big Three Conference...he also touched at some length on the Pacific war and asserted his government did not lightly undertake production and use of the terrible atomic bomb. The president said: 'We have used it in order to shorten the agony of war, in order to save many lives of young Americans.

Two American B-29 "Superfortress" bombers dropped the atomic bombs on Hiroshima and Nagasaki, Japan to end World War II in 1945. [LA CRESCENT AREA HISTORICAL SOCIETY ARCHIVES]

"...Concerning Europe, he said the war had indeed come home to Germany and the German people. He said 'It has come home in all the frightfulness with which the German leaders started and waged it. The German people are beginning to atone for the crimes of the gangsters whom they placed in power and whom they wholeheartedly approved and obediently followed. We are going to do what we can to make Germany over into a decent nation so that it may eventually work its way from economic chaos it has brought upon itself back into a safe and civilized world..."

Little did President Truman or anyone of the time know how the invention and use of the atomic bomb would shape world events still to come. The threat of using it has precariously maintained peace to an extent, though wars have occurred since then. The 1950s saw Americans preparing home bomb shelters during the Cold War. And ironically, no one in the world has felt as safe since the atomic bomb was used to bring peace.

Information from memorabilia donated to the La Crescent Historical Society by the Donald Frappier family.

CHAPTER 13:
SIGNS OF THE TIMES

RED SUN IN MORNING,
SAILORS TAKE WARNING...

Predicting the Weather by Nature

Even before radio and TV radar weather reports and forecasts, people had ways of predicting the weather for the day, month or even upcoming season by watching animals, weather patterns and "signs" in nature. Weather was an even bigger factor in daily life before modern weather predictions because most of the economy revolved around agriculture, so people paid attention. For instance, the weather during a full moon, according to previous generations, would indicate what type of weather to expect for the next month. So if it rained on a full moon, one could expect a month of rainy weather. In the short term, rings around the moon would indicate the coming of precipitation in the next few days.

But for long-term forecasts, people (especially farmers) paid attention to the "Ember Days" to reveal what the next season would be like. Ember Days are the Wednesday, Friday and Saturday of the last full week before the change of the season. They are said to predict the weather for the next three months. So just before the first day of spring, those three days will foretell what the months of spring will be like. The Wednesday would be the forecast for April, the Friday for May and the Saturday for June. Likewise with the three months of the other seasons. According to that theory, because of unusually warm Ember Days in September, the months of October, November and December of 2001 were all projected to be much warmer than normal, which they were.

Other signs of weather for the day follow:

- "Red sun in morning, sailor's take warning; Red sun at night, sailor's delight." (Red sun in morning would indicate stormy weather; at night a nice day the next day.)
- "Rain before 7, quit before 11."
- "If a chicken stays out in the rain, it will rain all day."
- "When your dog (or cat) eats grass it's going to rain."
- "When the cows run with their tails up it means rain."
- "If there is no dew on the grass it will rain."
- "If you see a spot of blue in the sky large enough to patch a pair of overalls, it will clear off and be a nice day."

Forecasts for a few days might include:

- "If the sun sets clear on a Friday night, it will rain or snow before Monday."
- "Sun dogs" (rainbow-like spots near the sun in the winter) indicate colder weather coming.

Longer term forecasts or forecasts of seasons:

- "When the robins return, they must be snowed on 3 times before spring is really here."
- "Rain on Easter Sunday brings rain the next 7 Sundays."
- "The first frost will occur 6 months after the first thunderstorm of spring."
- "When you hear the first cicada, it will be six weeks until frost."
- "Crickets singing in the house tell of a long cold winter."
- "Rolling thunder in the fall means a hard winter."

- "Large numbers of wooly caterpillars crossing the road from east to west means a hard winter is ahead."
- "If you have a white Thanksgiving, you'll have a black Christmas."
- "When snowdrifts face the North, spring will arrive early."

Crop forecasts:

- "Don't plant corn until the leaves on the walnut tree are as big as a squirrel's ear."
- "If it thunders on April Fool's Day it brings good crops of corn and hay."
- "When the wind is from the north-west on the day after spring it means good crops. If it is from the south-west, it means a dry summer."
- "When the hay in the fields leans to the north-east summer will be long and hot."

Fisherman's forecast:

1. "Wind from the east, fishing is least; wind from the west, fishing is best; wind from the North only fools go forth; wind from the South puts bait in their mouth."

Even with weather forecasting advanced with Dopler radar, it's still fun to see if the old ways of forecasting weather hold true, or if they're even *more* accurate than the forecasts the meteorologists give us!

Information from: *Ties That Bind* by Dysart, Iowa sixth-graders (1994) and from the author's grandmother (Hulda Christoph) and parents (Herbert and Marceile Christoph).

MAY I HAVE YOUR AUTOGRAPH?

Entries from a Victorian Era Autograph Book

"When you're at home
and over the tub
think of me before
you rub" – Your friend, Charlie Metcalf, Caledonia

"Friendship is a golden
Knot tied by an angel's hand" –
Yours Sincerely, Ella Eberhard, Mound Prairie

These are examples of some funny, serious and poetic thoughts from the friends and relatives of Julia Evans in her autograph book from March 24, 1883 until sometime in 1891. Such autographs can tell us not only who was in a particular area at a particular time – in their own handwriting – but also, the mood or thoughts of people at the time. One autograph was in a foreign language, possibly German, as it was written by Emma Tessmer in 1887. Several written by friends mention, "Remember the shop girls," indicating either some work-related or especially memorable incident. More selections from Julia's autograph book follow:

"The grain is God's bounty
and the flowers are his smiles" – Mr. C.A. Herzog, Hokah

"Remember me when far away
When only half awake
Remember me on your wedding day
And send me a piece of cake." – Your friend, Annie Zenner (?), Caledonia

"Remember twenty
five is the age ask
your ma" – T.W. Groff

The cover of a Victorian autograph book owned by J. F. Zisch of Dresbach, Minnesota in 1889. Autograph books were a popular way of remembering one's friends and relatives in the Victorian era. [LA CRESCENT AREA HISTORICAL SOCIETY ARCHIVES]

"May your joys be as deep
as the ocean,
your sorrows as light
as its foam." – Ever your friend, Marrion Ferguson,
La Crescent

"Scatter the sunbeams of kindness
Though your good deeds may never be known
The harvest will ripen in glory
If the seed be faithfully sown" – Your sincere friend,
Belle Weber, Caledonia

"A merry heart and smiling face
Are better far than sunny weather.
A noble life and forms of grace
Like leaves and flowers grow well together." –
Anna M. O'Riley

"In the golden chain of friendship
regard me as a link." –
Yours Sincerely, Lena Graf, Brownsville

"Droop not beneath disaster,
More sternly face the gales!
Thou yet mayst prove a master,
And o'er calm waters sail." –
Your Friend, Annie Brayton, La Crescent

"The Lord is my shepherd;
I shall not want." –
Your Friend, Charlotte Koehler Volkert, La Crescent

"The sun may lose its splendor
The tide may cease to flow.
The tyrants heart grow tender
And melt at others woe.
The frosty breath of December
May wilt the flowers of May
But ever I'll remember you dear Julia
Though I am far away." –
 Belle Eberhard Webster, Mound Prairie

"When twilight pulls the curtain
Down and pins it with a star
Remember you have still a friend
Though she is very far." –
 Your shop friend, Maime Cunningham, Caledonia

"I thought I thought
I thought in vain.
And so I thought
I'd write my name." –
Your friend, Geo. P. Riesland, Mound Prairie

"Let your days be bright and sunny
And your husband fat and funny." –
Yours Truly, Lydia Graben, Md. Prairie

"God never will forsake in need
the soul, that trusts in him indeed." –
Your Friend, Clara Moldenhauer

"Would that this garland fair
Might weave around thy life,
A spell to shield from care
A guard from every strife." –
A. Burrow, Mound Prairie

Though we didn't know Julia, these autographs give an indication of her friends and relatives and how they regarded her. It's a simple autograph book, but a fond remembrance.

From the autograph book of Julia Evans, 1883-1891.

SPEEDER CAUGHT
BY POLICEMAN ON BICYCLE

Area's First Automobile Speeder

"But officer, I was just getting the car up to speed to test it out..." Perhaps the excuse went something like that when the first automobile speeder was caught in La Crosse in 1907. The excuse doesn't work now, and it didn't then, either.

According to an old *La Crosse Tribune* the 1907 story went as follows:

Harry V. Pettigill, Minneapolis, demonstrator for the Buick Automobile Co., now attached to the Tanberg garage, 318 State, was fined $15 and costs in Judge Brindley's court for excessive speeding of an automobile yesterday afternoon at 6 o'clock, violating the new state law fixing 12 miles per hour as a maximum. Pettigill entered a plea of guilty and paid the fine.

A campaign to compel obedience of the state law has been started by Chief of Police Hugh H. Byrne, while the sane members of the automobile set in La Crosse are also behind the move to put a stop to speeding and endangering the lives of pedestrians and drivers of horses. Chief Byrne swore to the complaint against Pettigill while automobilists will swear to more if the laws relative to speed are violated further.

With the state license number hidden under the seat, Pettigill, with a party of three, fairly tore down State Street from the east. As the party whizzed by Central Police station, Chief Byrne ordered Detective John B. Webber to pursue.

Webber started on a bicycle and caught the autoists at the Hotel Stoddard where a stop was made. Pettigill, the driver, was arrested and the others allowed to go. He was brought to Central police station but liberated when a friend posted $25 bond.

Chief Byrne testified and swore Detective Webber

estimated the speed at 35 miles per hour. Pettigill admitted exceeding 12 miles but thought it about 18. He explained it was necessary to go faster to get the machine in condition to test it out.

'This is the first automobile case I have had', said Judge Brindley. 'The fine is $10 to $25 and ordinarily I would inflict the minimum expense for the first offense, but you were violating the law so flagrantly, and going so fast, that I cannot inflict the minimum fine. 'I fine you $15 and costs which will be $4.67.'

Automobilists in the courtroom who drive their machines at a moderate and sane rate of speed applauded Judge Brindley and promised to see that speed laws are enforced.

An automobile drives near the old Wagon Bridge that preceded the Cass Street Bridge across the Mississippi River into downtown La Crosse, Wisconsin from La Crescent, Minnesota c.1920s. The Wagon Bridge was replaced after it fell into the river in 1935 when it was struck by a car. [LA CRESCENT AREA HISTORICAL SOCIETY ARCHIVES]

Apparently, the temptation to speed is as old as the automobile. But, we'll have none of that wild speeding around here! Besides endangering people, you never know when a Policeman might catch you on his bicycle.

Information from 1907 *La Crosse Tribune* article.

LET THE MUSIC BEGIN
Brief History of Recorded Music

Did you know that the first machine to record music was made before the American Revolution? The history of recorded music dates back at least as far as the invention of the music box in Switzerland in 1770. It produced sound when metal pins set in a revolving barrel or disk plucked the tuned teeth of a steel comb.

It was more than 100 years before further advances were made in recorded music with Thomas Edison's invention of the cylinder phonograph in 1877, which he actually thought would be used as dictating machines in offices. The cylinders had indentations that created the sound with the needle or stylus moving over them.

"Platters," or flat 78-rpm (revolutions per minute) records, which were about ½ inch thick and recorded only on one side, were being developed about the same time by German-American, Emil Berliner. They had grooves for the needle to play the sound. They played much faster than the later 33 1/3- rpm long play albums or the 45-rpm single records of the 1950s – 1970s. By the 1930s records had music on both sides of the platter.

Surprisingly, piano rolls came *later*, and were quite popular and widely used on player pianos in the early 1900s. Piano rolls worked similarly to music boxes in player pianos with rolls of perforated paper.

In the latter half of the 20th century, recorded music changed to tapes with the invention of the 8-track tapes and players of the late 1960s, so people could listen to the recorded music of their choice in their moving cars. The tapes were magnetized to record and play sound.

By the mid-1970s music tapes had evolved into the smaller cassette tapes, with players that were portable, like the *Sony Walkman*, so people could listen to recorded music as they walked and exercised. This portable music player used with headphones could easily go anywhere, and not disturb other people.

CDs (compact discs) came into popular use in the 1990s with the development of digital recorded sound. It is also very portable, like the cassette, but uses lasers to read the microscopic pits and grooves of the discs.

Now, in the 2000s we have computer technology and the advent of digital music on tiny MP3 players, similar to the *Walkman.* The MP3s – actually mini computers – play music of the user's choice downloaded from computers or the Internet and hold a remarkable number of songs in a machine small enough to fit into the palm of the user's hand.

We can only guess how music will be recorded and played in the future!

Music boxes were the first form of recorded music. This music box was advertised as a "musical casket" in the October 25, 1883 *The Youth's Companion*. [THE YOUTH'S COMPANION – OCTOBER 25, 1883]

Information from Microsoft Encarta Encyclopedia and life experience by the author.

IF YOU KNEW SUSIE!

The Changing Moods of Recorded American Music

The 1920s were a time of tremendous social and technological change. Women finally won the right to vote; transportation and communications were entering a new era with the automobile, telephone, and the new invention of the radio becoming available to the masses. Not only was the world becoming more modern, but it was also seeming smaller as people could travel faster and learn quickly about what was going on in other parts of the U.S. and world. The world, which had remained largely unchanged for centuries, suddenly plunged into the age of technology, due in part to World War I.

Among the changes were hearing live or recorded music from far away in one's own home. No longer was it necessary to go somewhere to hear a band at an appointed time and place. The invention of the radio brought music to the people anywhere, anytime. The world would never be so silent again.

Because the radio could broadcast long distances, and because of the availability of phonographs and records, singers and bands that were featured on the radio stations became nationally known rather than remaining local talents. This not only propelled them into national stardom, but also gave the whole country something in common – the music. People all across the U.S. from New York City to the rural plains to the Rocky Mountains and to the West Coast all became united in a new way.

The music of each decade since says something about the mood of the country at the time. The 1920s ("Roaring Twenties") was the age of "Ragtime" music, as it was influenced by poor Black people. As ladies' hemlines went up, the music changed from sentimental, religious or ethnic, (due to the many immigrants) to anything goes; the dance craze swept across the country. Americans began to feel less like strangers and more like a united people.

The La Crescent Area Historical Society has recorded music from 1919 into the 1950s. Some old and scratchy 1920s hits include: "Swanee" by Al Jolson, who used to perform it in "black face" in 1920; the silly 1923 commentary on immigrants, "Yes! We Have No Bananas" by Billy Jones; the story of a wild girl in "If You Knew Susie" by Eddie Cantor from 1925; Sophie Tucker's "Some of These Days" from 1926, and several Paul Whitman Orchestra hits, including "Whispering."

With the onset of the Great Depression in the 1930s, the party atmosphere of the 1920s was over. The "Stein Song" from 1930 by Rudy Vallee was still as festive as a college fight song for a team before the reality of the Depression got into full swing. But then the music mellowed. Some oldies from the 1930s came from movies that allowed people to fanaticize about good times and being rich and carefree, such as the Fred Astaire dance movies of the time. Some of those hits include his romantic songs, "Cheek to Cheek" (1935) and "The Way You Look Tonight". Bing Crosby had hits with "Pennies From Heaven" in 1936, perhaps reflecting on the depressed economy, and a Hawaiian influence with "Sweet Leilani" from 1937. "A-tisket, A-tasket" was a popular song by Ella Fitzgerald in 1938, as was the ditzy 1939 hit, "Scatterbrain" by Frankie Masters & his Orchestra.

Other hits that transitioned from Ragtime to "Swing" and "Big Band" music from the 1930s were, "Happy Days Are Here Again" by Ben Selvin & his Orchestra, looking forward to better times; the cute song of honey-mooners in "Shuffle Off to Buffalo" by Hal Kemp and Skinnay Ennis; a song of heartbreak in "All of Me" by Paul Whitman & Mildred Bailey; "Goody Goody" by Benny Goodman and "Tiger Rag" by the Mills Brothers.

Sound had been added to the movies (they were initially known as "talkies") and many songs emerged from the motion pictures as big hits: "The Continental" by Leo Reisman from the 1934 movie, *The Gay Divorcee*; "Jeepers Creepers" by Al Donahue from *Going Places*;

Rudy Vallee -- heart-throb of 1920s women -- graces the cover of this sheet music for "Good Night Sweetheart" from that era. Ever evolving, American's taste in music seems to change with the times. [COURTESY OF DONNA HUEGEL]

"Lullaby of Broadway" by the Dorsey Brothers from *Gold Diggers* in 1935; "Thanks for the Memory" in 1938 from *The Big Broadcast of 1938* and Judy Garland's classic "Over the Rainbow" from *The Wizard of Oz* in 1939.

The 1940s saw more "big bands" with energetic "Swing" music to set the toes a-tapping and keep up the morale of the soldiers and their families during World War II. Before America was in the war, Kate Smith sang "The Last Time I Saw Paris" from the 1941 movie *Lady Be Good*. The song was sentimental and nostalgic. During WWII Glenn Miller had everyone up and dancing to his many hits, which included, "In the Mood," "Moonlight Serenade," and "Pennsylvania 6-5000." Bing Crosby had one of the largest selling records of all time with "White Christmas" that brought tears of longing for home from the G.I.s and their families. The song was from the 1942 movie, *Holliday Inn.* He had another hit with the movie song, "Swinging on a Star" from the 1944 production *Going My Way*. Meanwhile, rival Frank Sinatra, singing with the Tommy Dorsey Orchestra, was making girls swoon to his hits with his mellow, romantic voice. Among them was "I'll Be Seeing You," a song about soldiers leaving for duty and looking forward to coming home. And trying to keep hope for better times alive was his song "There Are Such Things." Girls certainly must have thought about being Frank's girlfriend in the romantic "Polka Dots and Moonbeams," and when he sang the praises of a girl named "Delores."

The Andrews Sisters' sweet harmonies had multiple hits including the snappy "Boogie Woogie Bugle Boy," the song about a musician drafted into the Army during World War II; the lively "Pennsylvania Polka" and "Rum and Coca-Cola" with a Jamaican theme and sound.

Other songs reflecting the war front were: "Praise the Lord and Pass the Ammunition" by Kay Keyser; "Commin' in on a Wing and a Prayer" by the Song Spinners, and "When the Lights Go on Again (All Over the World)" by Vaughn Monroe, underscoring "black-outs" by covering windows so no light would show from buildings at night, so they would not be easy targets for bomber planes. A song that reflected a G.I.'s fear that his girlfriend might replace him was titled: "Somebody Else is Taking My Place" by Russ Morgan. Then there was the comical Spike Jones and His City Slickers, who were known for their funny songs such as "Der Fuehrer's Face," making fun of Hitler and the Nazis.

Music of World War II also reflected the dilemmas on the home front, and families and sweethearts longing for their soldiers at war with songs like: "They're Either Too Young or Too Old" by Jimmy Dorsey and Kitty Kallen, which lamented the dating problem for women with men their age away at the war. Doris Day sang "Sentimental Journey" in 1944. The Harry James Orchestra did the soulful song "You Made Me Love You" and "It's Been a Long, Long Time," with Kitty Kallen singing in a longing, lustful way about continuing a romance when the soldiers returned home.

The 1950s saw a variety in music as the "Baby Boom" was in full swing with G.I.s returned home and married. It was a time of family, prosperity, fun, and a youthful movement of teen love and angst. Perhaps no song expressed the much longed for idyllic home life of the previous decade better than "Mockin' Bird Hill" by Les Paul and Mary Ford. Meanwhile, Rosemary Clooney sang "Hey There," giving motherly advice to young lovers.

Love songs were abundant with the likes of Patti Page's soft "Allegheny Moon" and "Tennessee Waltz." Many more love songs with a lovesick tone by the Platters included "My Prayer," "The Magic Touch," and "Only You." A light look at being in love came through with Dean Martin's "That's Amore." A few tunes with subtle lust also became hits: "Blueberry Hill," where Fats Domino "found his thrill;" "Standing On the Corner" – "watchin' all the girls go by" and proclaiming, "Buddy, you can't go to jail for what you're thinkin'" by The Four Lads; and Peggy Lee's sexy "Fever."

Perry Como had numerous hits in the 1950s ranging from

dramatic and crooning love songs, to reverent religious songs, to fun melodies of "Hot Diggitty (Dog Ziggitty Boom)," "Catch a Falling Star," and a Cuban influenced "Papa Loves Mambo." Meanwhile, The Coasters concentrated more on the teen crowd with hits like "Charlie Brown," who was always getting picked on; "Poison Ivy," warning of a girl who'll "get under your skin," teen angst with "Young Blood," and dealing with demanding adults in "Yakkety-Yak" (don't talk back!).

But the 1950s music also pointed toward the future with artists like Little Richard heating things up with "Tutti Frutti," Chuck Berry's "Johnny B. Goode," and of course, the King of Rock 'N Roll, Elvis Presley belting out the new sounds of "Jail House Rock" and "You Ain't Nothin' But a Hound Dog!" After that, teen music skewed from that of adults, which made it all the more appealing to the teenagers.

And so it goes with each generation coming up with the sounds of their times.

Information from a critical review of a variety of records, tapes and CD's of music from different eras by the author, and life experience.

CHAPTER 14:
HAPPY HOLIDAYS

ROSES ARE READ, VIOLETS ARE BLUE...
Valentine Verses From the Early 1900s

The custom of sending valentines has been going on for a long time. What were valentines like in the romantic era of the Titanic? A sampling from the archives follows.

A 1910 valentine postcard featured a picture of a man down on his knees, pleading to a beautiful woman in a long gown and feathered hat, and had a verse entitled "The Bluff"— It went like this:

> "I'll go and jump into the sea,
> I'll go into a slow decline,
> I'll go and do some reckless thing
> If you don't be my Valentine."

A postcard from 1912 showing a Victorian-dressed little girl holding a big heart from cupid had a verse that went as follows:

> "The best I have I sent to thee,
> I hope this heart will capture thee."

An undated valentine of the era, picturing a snickering girl with her bulldog and a scared boy proclaimed:

> "Though I keep guarded all the time
> This loving heart of mine,
> Don't be afraid and run away,
> You are my Valentine."

Everything you could want in a valentine. This postcard valentine is postmarked 1910.
[LA CRESCENT AREA HISTORICAL SOCIETY ARCHIVES]

Some of the old valentines have pictures surrounded by white paper lace on the cover and open to a cartoon drawing of children in a romantic setting, such as on a picnic, with a sweet sentiment:

"This valentine I send to you
Just to prove my love is true
There's nothing more that I can say
Except, I love you more each day."

There were a few homemade valentines of construction paper, featuring red hearts and picture cutouts of flowers and dolls. One of these undated valentines seemed to be from around 1918 since the dolls pictured together were dressed as a nurse, sailor and soldier in World War I era attire. One of these valentines included the time-tested verse of:

"Roses are red, violets are blue,
Sugar is sweet and so are you."

A lovely undated card showing a house surrounded by flowers contained the sentiments of a shy person as it stated within:

"I'm so bashful!
The Valentine's a fine invention
For bashful chaps like me,
I need not even sign my name
A great relief, you see."

A 1911 valentine picturing a cartoon of lady and gentlemen cats had the gentleman cat tipping his hat to the lady, with the sentiment:

"I'll lay down my Nine Lives for you…"

A valentine from 1926 was the shape of a car with two riders within and a cupid on top. It merely said:

"You – Auto be my Valentine."

Not all the valentine greetings were of love, however. An insightful postcard from 1910 showed a dressmaker labeled "Miss Fitt Dressmaker." The verse accompanying it read:

"When the dressmaker comes for a stay,
She is generally paid by the day;
She'll ruin a skirt,
'Fits well,' she'll assert, --
Gives excuses galore for delay!"

Kids' valentines today are a far cry from those of a century ago, with today's often reflecting pop culture with what personality, toy or cartoon is in vogue, and less sincere in the message. It's doubtful people a hundred years ago could have even imagined "scratch & sniff" valentines!

Information from valentines donated by Norma Wetzel, Olive Dacey Gershon and Marion Evans.

PUT ON YOUR EASTER BONNET
Easter Fashions of 1881

There's an old song called the *"Easter Parade"* that croons, "Put on your Easter bonnet with all the frills upon it; and you will be the fairest in the Easter Parade…" That's something we rarely see anymore. But the *Godey's Lady's Book and Magazine*, 1881, gives an idea of Easter fashions of the well to do at that time.

Hats were described as "hat of Milan braid trimmed with plaid gauze, blue and pink, and flowers." Another was a "black straw hat, the edge finished by a narrow embroidered band; it is trimmed with black satin and shaded red feathers." Also described was a "Tuscan straw bonnet trimmed with old gold and blue satin and feathers. The brim is faced [*Note: finished*] with satin."

Easter bonnet fashions of 1881. [GODEY'S LADY'S BOOK AND MAGAZINE – 1881]

It was noted that hats of this year would feature "large flowers used in wreaths of a single color, but several shades, such as palest pink to darkest damask red; or cream to deepest yellow." A remark followed: "Floral monstrosities are to be avoided."

Ladies dresses once again were made with an abundance of material in intricate designs and frills. The "hour-glass" shape of a thin waist remained in style, necessitating the use of tight corsets, which girls began wearing at the age of 11 to begin to form the shape the men admired. Some wealthy families in the East even went so far as to have doctors surgically remove a couple of the girls' ribs when they were young, so they could have the desired thin waist of the day – 12 inches or so! The restrictive corsets in turn necessitated the use of ladies' fans and the popularity of "fainting couches," as the fashions made it difficult for the women to breathe.

Comments on the dresses stated that some of the dress designs were "reproductions of designs used 100 years ago." The colors in fashion for the year were taken directly from America: "Indian pink of the far West, the palm-tree of the South, and the autumn leaves of the American forests, have been carried to French manufacturers," the book stated.

Children's clothes for both boys and girls were just below the knee in length, with knickers for the boys and skirts for the girls. Their footwear was similar... high tops buttoned along the side with noticeable heel. Young boys' dress-up fashions were as likely as girls' to have bows, pleats and even lace.

Men's fashions were not included in the book.

We rarely even see hats other than baseball caps these days, or maybe the red hats of the new "Red Hat Society" ladies. Yet a pretty hat is as likely now as then to draw attention and compliments. And some of us still enjoy wearing them.

Information from 1881 *Godey's Ladys Book and Magazine* and from information from tour guides at historic Forestville, Minnesota.

GHOST OF CHRISTMAS PAST
A Century-Old Christmas Tragedy

Among the early newspaper clippings of local murders, obituaries of John S. Harris, and stories of humor and misfortune in the *Apple Country Chronicles* of the La Crescent Area Historical Society is the following story of a La Crescent Christmas tragedy from over a hundred years ago. It is the strange story of Charles Zink's disappearance in La Crescent the day before Christmas. The story as written follows:

DEAD THREE MONTHS
AND THE BODY IN THE HOUSE
UNKNOWN TO THE FAMILY

A shocking discovery was made late Tuesday afternoon in an upper room of the old hotel at La Crescent. On the lower floor lives Mrs. Charles Zink and her seven children. For three months she had been living with the belief that her husband had deserted her; but it now develops that not only was he dead and she a widow all this time, but that she had been in the same house with his lifeless body ever since he disappeared. The last seen of Zink alive was on the 24th of December, when he left the house, saying he was going out to look for work. Nobody saw him return and nothing was heard of him. The second story of the house, where Mrs. Zink resides, is untenanted and Mr. D. Cameron, who owns it went there Tuesday to open the upper rooms. One of the doors was locked. Procuring a key he tried to open it but a weight on the other side prevented. Through the crack he saw the arm of a man, and, securing some assistance, forced open the door. There on the floor lay the body of Zink. The cord around his neck told the story.

He had fastened one end of the rope to the door knob and then sunk down as far as it would let him and was strangled. This evidently happened about Christmas when he disappeared.

A coroner's inquest was held yesterday and a verdict rendered that he had died by his own hand.

There is a Charles Zink listed in La Crescent cemetery files of 1895, but no cemetery plot listed. So, it is thought he was buried in a pauper's grave. It is believed the survivors moved away.

Information from the *Apple Country Chronicles*, a publication of the La Crescent Area Historical Society.

A SPECIAL CHRISTMAS PRESENT

A Christmas Story from the McGuffy Reader

The following Christmas story is written as published in the 1879 *McGuffy's Second Eclectic Reader*:

The picture that accompanied the Christmas story in the McGuffy Reader of 1879 in the 1920 revised edition. [MCGUFFY'S SECOND ECLECTIC READER – REVISED EDITION – 1920]

MAMMA'S PRESENT

1. Jessie played a good joke on her mamma. This is the way she did it.
2. Jessie had gone to the woods with Jamie and Joe to get green branches to trim up the house for Christmas. She wore her little cap, her white furs, and her red leggings.
3. She was a merry little girl, indeed; but she felt sad this morning because her mother had said, "The children will all have Christmas presents, but I don't expect any for myself. We are too poor this year."

4.   When Jessie told her brothers this, they all talked about it a great deal. "Such a good, kind mamma and no Christmas present! It's too bad."

5.   "I don't like it," said little Jessie, with a tear in her eye.

6.   "Oh, she has you," said Joe.

7.   "But I am not something new," said Jessie.

8.   "Well, you will be new, Jessie," said Joe, "when you get back. She has not seen you for an hour."

9.   Jessie jumped and laughed. "Then put me in the basket, and carry me to mamma, and say, 'I am her Christmas present.'"

10.   So they set her in the basket, and put green branches all around her. It was a jolly ride. They set her down on the doorstep, and went in and said, "There's a Christmas present out there for you, mamma."

11.   Mamma went and looked, and there, in a basket of green branches, sat her own little laughing girl.

12.   "Just the very thing I wanted most," said mamma.

13.   "Then, dear mamma," said Jessie, bounding out of her leafy nest, "I should think it would be Christmas for mammas all the time, for they see their little girls every day."

Just a little reminder from the past that people often forget in our materialistic society at Christmas time, what the best gifts really are.

Information from 1879 *McGuffy's Second Eclectic Reader.*

Not all Christmas cards of the past featured nativity, winter or Santa Claus pictures. This Christmas card c. early 1900s features poet John Greenleaf Whittier and one of his poems. [LA CRESCENT AREA HISTORICAL SOCIETY ARCHIVES]

LET THE GAMES BEGIN

1881 Christmas Auction Game

Are you stumped for holiday entertainment for a party or gathering? Here's an idea perhaps your ancestors may have used for holiday fun in 1881. Using real money, it could also be a fun holiday fundraiser today.

The idea was published in the 1881 *Godey's Lady's Book and Magazine*. It was called "The Christmas Auction." The article also tells of a slower pace of life, and that cheating in some instances may not have been taken so seriously. Instructions follow as written in the book. (Keep in mind, writers of the day didn't believe in lots of paragraphs.)

It goes like this:

The following game will furnish work for the many idle hands that at this holiday time are seeking an easy job with lots of fun in it. All sorts of useless trifles are gathered together, with as many articles of value as can be afforded to the common stock, and are each wrapped in paper, so that the packages cannot be distinguished from each other. Cards are then marked in duplicate, giving a price for each, one card being attached to each package, and the other being kept for current use. At the proper time, a general auction is held of all the packages, the duplicate cards being distributed among the guests. The appointed auctioneer displays each bundle in turn, and ignorant of its contents, describes it with a showman's eloquence, and finally relinquishes it to the person holding the duplicate card. The purchaser and the auctioneer are often equally sold in the transition, which may become very amusing under the hands of an expert salesman. The frolic may be made still more exciting by putting no price upon the articles, and allowing them to be sold to the highest bidder. The competition will then become fast and furious, and is limited only by the funds of the bidders. This money can be supplied in quantity by cutting coins in card or paper, and marking them at their value. The making of correct change, and the occasional attempts at cheating, then add to the amusement arising from the consternation which frequently attends the opening of the purchased bundle, or the amazement expressed at the worth or worthlessness of the contents.

The pace of life may have been slower in our ancestors' days and they had to work hard, but they also knew how to have fun together. It sounds like fun. Does anyone want to play?

Information from 1881 *Godey's Lady's Book and Magazine.*

MINCEMEAT, ANYONE?
Victorian Christmas Recipes

Have you ever read an old Christmas story that mentioned mincemeat or plum pudding, and you wondered what it would taste like? As it turns out, some recipes for mincemeat call for meat, and some don't. And, ironically, plum pudding contains no plums. If you'd like to try them out for a special Christmas treat, here are two recipes from the Victorian era.

Old-Fashioned Mincemeat
4 quarts tart apples (pared and chopped)
1 orange (finely ground)
3 cups raisins (ground)
3 cups whole raisins
4 quarts green tomatoes (ground)
½ -pound beef suet (optional)
2 cups strong coffee
3-½ cups brown sugar
2 tablespoons cinnamon
1-1/2 teaspoons nutmeg
¼ cup vinegar
1-1/2 teaspoons salt
1-1/2 teaspoons cloves
Juice of one lemon

Grind washed tomatoes and cook in own juice 5 minutes. Drain. Add chopped apples, ground orange, and ground raisins. Bring to a boil. Add whole raisins and coffee. Add rest of ingredients and cook at least 35 minutes until thickened. Seal in hot jars.

Christmas Plum Pudding
1 cup suet, ground
1 cup raisins
1 cup currants
1 cup molasses

1 cup sweet milk
1 lemon (juice and rind grated)
1 teaspoon soda dissolved in 1/8 cup hot water
3-1/4 cups flour
   Mix thoroughly. Put into large fruit cans filled ¾ full. Steam in large kettle of boiling water. Set cans on rack in bottom. Cover and boil water for 2-1/4 to 3 hours. Serve hot with lemon-flavored hard sauce.

Recipes from the past can enlighten us not only about the tastes and diets of our ancestors, but also about what food was available, and even the technology of the time. For instance, there were no oven temperatures listed for recipes until the early 1900s since there were no temperature gauges on stoves, mostly heated with wood.

Oven temperatures, if listed were for a "slow" (warm, not hot) oven, "moderate" or "hot" oven. The baker gauged the oven temperature strictly by feel. Temperatures called "moderate" meant you could stick your hand in the oven for a few moments without burning it; and a "hot" oven meant you had to pull your hand out of the oven right away from the intense heat.

Measurements before the 1900s were often less scientific, with measurements by the "gill" (equal to ¼ pint), teacup, pound, quart, pinch, etc. instead of today's standardized cups and spoons by fractions of sizes.

Victorian recipes from an 1881 *Godey's Lady's Book and Magazine* include: Temperance Cake, Hare Soup, Lobster Croquettes, Calf's Foot Broth, Hasty Pudding, Pickled Tripe, Pigs Head Cheese, Blackberry Cordial, Pate De Foie Gras, Shanghai Curry, Indian Suet Pudding, Quail Pie, Potted Pigeons, Huckleberry Pudding, Rice Cakes, Spitchcock Eels, Lamb Pie, Tomato Ketchup and a wedding cake that used 40 eggs and 5 pounds of raisins among the ingredients.

Cooking or baking directions in these old recipes are often amusing by today's standards. Some recipes take not only many hours, but even *weeks* to complete. And occasionally, the cook adds comments. Still, experience with cooking this way, and periodic checking for color, runniness or tenderness of the food being baked or cooked provided good food in the hands of a good cook or baker, despite the lack of high technology.

Recipes from the past also give us a peek into the kitchens of homes of years gone by. They are a little glimpse of the life of our ancestors.

Information from 1881 *Godey's Lady's Book and Magazine* and Recipes from 1881 Cookbook from the La Crescent Area Historical Society.

ALL I WANT FOR CHRISTMAS IS...

Things for Christmas – 1883

My grandma told me about Christmas when she was a poor immigrant child in North Dakota about a century ago. It seemed more like Thanksgiving than the Christmas we know today. She said they all went to church and sang Christmas carols and got an apple or an orange as a treat. The focus was on church, a nice dinner, and celebration with family, friends and neighbors.

The next generation did the same, but children got a toy for Christmas as well. My generation did the same, but kids got more toys from Santa, with less emphasis on the religious aspect. This generation...well, you know how it is. Still, in 1883, there were things to be bought and given if you had the money. Examples from *The Youth's Companion* catalog of 1883 follow:

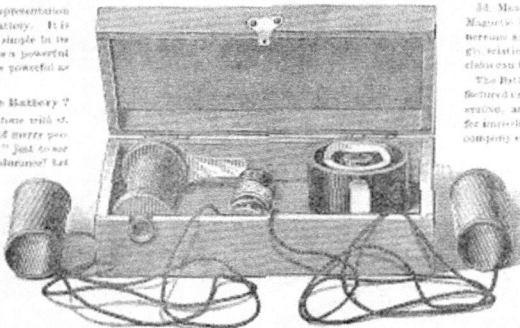

An Electro-magnetic battery was one of the Christmas items pictured for sale in the 1883 *The Youth's Companion* magazine. It carried items selected from the Catalogue of Cassell & Co. Ltd. of New York. [THE YOUTH'S COMPANION – OCTOBER 25, 1883]

Men and boys always seem to like gadgets and technology. The latest technology at the time was the "electro-magnetic battery". It was so new, in fact, that they weren't sure what to do with it yet. The advertisement stated, "Although simple in its construction, yet it produces a powerful current of electricity..." It added, "What can I do with the Battery? First, you can have a good time with it. Have you ever seen a group of merry people gather around a 'Battery' just to see the fun and test their own endurance? Let a group of young people join hands, then pass a current of electricity through, and you will soon see who has the strongest nerve." Other suggested uses were to make money with it as an attraction, to use at school to teach the principles of electricity, or medical use to relieve symptoms of "nervous affection, rheumatism, neuralgia, sciatica, and toothache."

There was also the "Improved Business Telephone" which advertised as two transmitters with 300 feet of wire. It said, "This Telephone will articulate clearly one thousand feet. We know of persons who use it successfully a distance of one mile." The ad suggested using it on the farm between the house and barn or field, for the manufacturer between his home and factory, or likewise for the merchant to keep in touch with his store when he wasn't there, or even for fun between friends and neighbors.

There were no movies yet, but you could get a "Magic Lantern with views, lectures and seventy-four tickets" to put on a show and make some money. Of course, there was no electricity yet, so the views were projected in a dark room by kerosene lantern light. Among the views were, "accurate portraits of Longfellow, Whittier, Bryant, Holmes and Tennyson, with a short sketch of the life of each, the story of 'The Lazy Ant' in three chapters, 'The Gobbler Gobbled', 'The Singing Lesson', 'Crossing the Ferry', 'Welcome' and 'Goodnight'." Ten German views on glass were said to be "very pleasing. They are beautifully painted in bright colors and represent a variety of subjects, both comic and landscape."

An ad for Columbia Bicycles (for men) and Tricycles for women (that were more like wheelchairs with the third wheel in the back for balance, pedals in front, and steering handles on the sides) focused on the healthful benefits on cycling. "Two things" it said, "are needful in the animal economy: to supply the blood with nutriment, and to rid it of excretion. Exercise is a powerful aid to the latter process; oxygen is indispensable to the former one. Bicycling supplies both." – *Medical Brief.*

Other mechanical and entertainment items included a crude telegraph, steam engines, a caligraph writing machine, (what we would call a typewriter) and a stereoscope with stereoscopic views. And there were guns and knives for the men folk.

In the section of "Articles for Family Use" was an ad for a book entitled, *What to Get for 100 Breakfasts*. A sample breakfast was "Hominy and Milk. Beef Steak. Flour and Indian Waffles, Baked Apple Sauce. Coffee. Ripe Fruit." Some other book titles were: *Little Women*, *Tennyson's Poems*, *Bible Scenes and Stories*, *Shakespeare's Complete Works*, and *Pilgrim's Progress*.

Other things for women included jewelry, silverware, a sewing machine, a "musical casket" (music box), wood fueled cooking range, corsets, wigs (also for men), boot buttoner, macramé and crochet instructions, vases and an "odor barrel" (perfume dispenser in the shape of a keg).

More things for the family and children included: card games such as "Authors," "Old Maid," "Snap," and others; toy tea sets, dolls, ring toss, autograph books, photograph albums and assorted children's books. There were also games with names like "American Fire Department," "Centennalia," and "Popping the Question." And of course, there were ice skates and roller skates (all were the clamp-on kind). Roller skates were for the sidewalks or rinks. And there were a number of musical instruments ranging from flutes, harmonicas, guitars and banjos, to violins, accordions and an organ, as before the invention of radio or other recorded music, people entertained themselves and one another by making their own music.

Recipients probably treasured many of the gifts of 1883. In time, many gifts were probably taken for granted, or tucked away to be forgotten for a while. But even today, many of the gifts of 1883 would be treasured items.

Information from 1883 *The Youth's Companion* catalog and from my grandmother, Hulda Christoph

ABOUT THE AUTHOR

A native of New Hampton, Iowa, Donna Christoph Huegel is a writer, artist and archivist at the La Crescent Area Historical Society since she started the organization's archives in 1993. After attending Mount Mercy College and the University of Iowa, she has been writing for over 30 years, being published in the *Tulsa World Herald, Des Moines Register* and *Milwaukee Journal.* She currently writes historical articles for the *Houston County News.* She authored *Many a Grove and Orchard—The Story of John S. Harris* and contributed stories and a poem to the anthology, *America's Heartland Remembers—Words and Pictures Before During and After September 11, 2001.* A volunteer in school, church and community for over 25 years, she was instrumental in naming a local park for Minnesota's first apple grower, John S. Harris; placing a maker at a local cemetery for unknown victims of the 1874 diphtheria epidemic; and using her artistic skill to paint a mural and do decorative work to help save the historic Concordia Ballroom in La Crosse, Wisconsin from closing. Ms. Huegel is listed in the 2004 *Who's Who of American Women.* She lives with her husband, Len, near La Crescent, Minnesota. They have two grown sons, Eric and Ryan.